The Frenchman and the Seven Deadly Sins

The Frenchman and the Seven Deadly Sins

by FERNANDO DIAZ-PLAJA

Translated by ERNST SCHRADER

Illustrations by CYRIL SATORSKY

CHARLES SCRIBNER'S SONS / NEW YORK

Copyright © 1972 Fernando Diaz-Plaja

Spanish language edition ©Fernando Diaz-Plaja
Alianza Editorial, S.A. Madrid, 1969

This book published simultaneously in the United States of America and in Canada-
Copyright under the Berne Convention

All rights reserved.
No part of this book may be reproduced in any form
without the permission of Charles Scribner's Sons.

A-8.72[H]

Printed in the United States of America
Library of Congress Catalog Card Number 72–496
SBN 684–12928–0 (cloth)

Contents

    Preface   *vii*
1. *Pride*   1
2. *Avarice*   45
3. *Lust*   65
4. *Anger*   101
5. *Gluttony*   117
6. *Envy*   137
7. *Sloth*   145

Preface

France looms large in the imagination of Americans. Without the help of French troops and the munitions forwarded by France and Spain, the thirteen embattled colonies might have struggled against Great Britain in vain, and the Marquis de Lafayette is remembered with a love rivaling that reserved for Washington himself. This early romance between the two countries was interrupted by the French Revolution and the Napoleonic Wars, but with the return of peace, America's heart began to yearn once more for Paris.

Henry James, Ernest Hemingway, Gertrude Stein, and Langston Hughes are representative of the many American luminaries who lived for various periods in Paris. Every year thousands of their countrymen fly or sail to the City of Light to renew their acquaintance with beauty, fashion, and the delights appropriate to a civilized body and mind.

This book is the testimony of a Spaniard, an ardent, though occasionally rueful, admirer of France. Spain

PREFACE

shares borders with two countries, but one—Portugal—is just another road to the Atlantic, which we can reach equally well from Galicia or western Andalusia. France, on the other hand, is our only land-pass to the rest of Europe, and even though airplanes have now given us the luxurious option of skipping over countries, we find it perfectly natural to begin our explorations of the continent on the other side of the Pyrenees.

For centuries everything that was modern in Spain arrived by way of France. A person who drove a car was called a chauffeur for years, and Charlie Chaplin was known as "Charlot," the nickname the French have given to every Charles except General de Gaulle. This friendly borrowing from a wealthier neighbor was at times punctuated by friction and the marching back and forth of troops, to the point where seventeenth-century commentators spoke casually of "the natural antipathy between Spaniards and Frenchmen," but certain regions of Spain have traditionally felt particularly friendly toward France. In Catalonia, where I put in my first years of college, the intellectual climate has always been pro-French, and under its influence I read Mauriac, Maurois, Duhamel, and Baudelaire before I got to Unamuno or Machado. My first book and my doctoral thesis both dealt with French history.

So much for my bookish credentials. I went to France as soon as the difficulties arising from the Spanish Civil War and the Second World War would permit. From my first visit in 1948 until today, I have never let two years go by without crisscrossing France in as many directions as I could, by rail and by car, from Hendaye to the Belgian frontier, from Cherbourg to Cerbère, from Bordeaux to Strasbourg. Whenever possible, I abandoned the superhighways to follow the well-paved, more peaceful secondary roads connecting one small town with another, where the church, a centuries-old castle, the equally traditional *épicerie, boucherie,* and *boulangerie* shops, and their clientele combine to form the backbone of French society.

PREFACE

In the capital itself I have sought to discover the ancient genius of the country in the city's older quarters, museums, and libraries, while I have looked for its modern spirit on the quays of the Seine, the shelves of its bookstores, and the offerings of its movie houses and theaters. In elegant restaurants and shadowy bars, in conversations with a duchess or philosophic or jesting beggars, in neighborhood parks and ostentatious squares, in Notre Dame and the Place Pigalle, I have explored a thousand facets of the incomparable city. Many times I was tired physically, but never in spirit. As President John Kennedy observed, all men have two countries, one where they were born, the other Paris.

Paris receives such a disproportionate amount of attention in the world that the French constantly debate its role: "France is not just its capital," we are reminded. Possibly so, but clearly the large majority of things that the world considers French come from Paris, and the city has usurped the job of representing the entire country. Is it unfair to go along with this pretension? I'm not sure; a situation that has existed for so many centuries acquires a kind of legitimacy of its own. When a part of something attracts more attention than the whole, the reason may be that the part has more character and personality: this is true of Andalusia, which symbolizes Spain to outsiders, though few people elsewhere in the country play the castanets.

Paris has added immeasurably to the style and zest of French civilization, but the rest of France is not without interest. The provinces, almost always lovely, their cities asleep in the shadow of a Gothic cathedral, with tree-lined avenues paced by venerable citizens with white mustaches and the red ribbon of the Legion of Honor in their lapels, provide welcome relief for the traveler whose vision is jaded and whose legs are weary from walking the streets of Paris. This relief need not be extended, however, since in a few days it can become tiresome.

This fabulous world, the world of Paris and the prov-

PREFACE

inces and the entire French nation, I have tried to explore in this book, following the plan laid out earlier in my books about Spain and the United States. Here, then, as best I can interpret it, is the attitude of the average Frenchman toward the seven deadly sins.

FERNANDO DIAZ-PLAJA

1 Pride

NATIONAL PRIDE

The name of the book or, rather, short essay, is *Réflexions sur la singularité d'être français,* and it was written by the famous French novelist Roger Vailland. Neither the title nor the topic surprised anyone in France. For the fact is, being French is a unique experience; it is—let's admit it at the outset—marvelous.

The feeling of greatness is strengthened when one's neighbors are little. In the case of France, the countries around her try hard to bring this optical effect into play. The intellectual elites of Spain, Italy, Switzerland, and

PRIDE

Belgium have long been admirers and imitators of the French style in literature and the fashion passing for art—an imitation that occasionally reached the point of national treason, as with the Spanish Francophiles in 1808, when Napoleon invaded Spain. At the other end of Europe, in Russia, it was considered very elegant to speak French (as in the novels of Tolstoy) and the aristocrats employed it among themselves, using Russian only to speak to serfs and servants. Even today in Rumania and Bulgaria I have encountered elderly gentlemen, almost always anti-Communist, who relished the chance to use the language they learned as children in the best schools of Bucharest or Sofia.

As for Germany, the country that has been the hardest of all on France and her enemy for generations, its deep admiration is transformed every twenty years into an irresistible desire to violate her. Like a timid man in love, Germany cannot declare its feelings to the object of its adoration, nor does it dare imitate her language and fashions, for fear of being called a snob. One fine day, however, after living with its frustration for years, it throws itself upon her to rape and strangle her if necessary (see Lust). But that there is admiration in all this one can't possibly doubt. The most beautiful testimonial ever made to France originated with the German *vox populi;* a standard German idiom used to describe a marvelous personal situation is that one finds oneself *als Gott in Frankreich,* "like God in France."

But, some will say, all that is past. France today, without its empire, with all its economic problems, rescued from two defeats by American aid, cannot possibly presume as it did before, and must have dropped its haughty airs. Besides, the age of nationalism is over, and in its place we have the idea of Europe....

Sensible thoughts, but inaccurate in the French case, and perhaps in others. As soon as de Gaulle presented himself on the political rostrum again, all the old and noble topics were revived. *Grandeur* came back in fashion, the "destiny of France" recovered its place in public pronouncements, political and economic independence began to seem a possible goal, France walked out of NATO, developed its deterrent force, exploded atomic devices. . . .

These events and attitudes were so ancient and outmoded that the French became quite ironic about de Gaulle and his "notions." Newspaper cartoons, the talk in Parisian cafés and salons, and the songs and jokes of comedians in the cabarets and theaters of the country concurred in regarding the rhetoric of the day as old, worn out, and laughable. But in the hour of truth, at the ballot box, for eleven long years the French voted overwhelmingly for the man who offered them what had remained, like a ray of hope, in the soul of every Frenchman: *la gloire*.

French political history of the last hundred years has been marked by a curious equilibrium between the two most obvious propensities found in the average Frenchman: love of glory and respect for reason. Since these impulses are almost always contradictory, they must be alternated. The first is fired up until it becomes necessary, as well as logical and humane, to pursue the second. Algeria is an example. France was obligated by her glorious history and her moral commitment to the colonists of that region of Africa to stay there forever. Reason, of course, counseled the opposite. Decolonization was going forward all over the world and it was impossible to fight against the current. Typical of the duality in the situation, the very same man who had inflamed the hearts of the French with his patriotic addresses was the one who made the realistic decision to abandon Algeria and with it the largest part of the old French empire.

As in a fairy tale, this good deed was rewarded: the states made newly independent raised the number of French-speaking nations in the United Nations to thirty-three, counting those for which French is the official language and those that use it in cultural and business affairs. A language that had fallen rapidly in prestige and importance after the war (giving way to English) returned to fashion.

In the events of May 1968, something similar occurred. The rebellious students seemed only too French, with their slogans ranging from obscenities to good literature (about this particular obsession we shall say more later) as, for example, the phrases "Power to the imagination!" or "Be realistic: demand the impossible." Barricades were thrown up in the streets, just as in the time of the Commune. (Minister of Culture André Malraux noted the anachronism of raising barricades, a nineteenth-century defense against cavalry charges, now that the state no longer employs that force.) French passion held sway, the hearts of all were swollen with brilliant phrases, yet the revolution was marred by few deaths (none in Paris, three in Lyon), and a few months later it was snuffed out by the votes of the immense majority of Frenchmen.

Many who voted this way were, at the outset, completely in accord with the revolutionaries and felt irked at the paternalistic and faintly disdainful way de Gaulle treated them. I was astonished to hear Frenchmen expressing antigovernment sentiments in luxury hotels on Spain's Costa del Sol in the first days of the movement. A little later, these worthy citizens, along with those who had always been on the Right, voted for law and order. Perhaps the same factors, differing only in timing, obliged them to vote the opposite way in 1969. Their citizenly pride could no longer tolerate de Gaulle's haughty insistence that they reaffirm every few years that they adored him and could not live without him. Even so, ten million voted for him as opposed to eleven million against.

The immense patriotism of the French shows up, more than anywhere else, in their treatment of their national history. Every country has a skeleton in the closet: Spain has the Inquisition, the United States its treatment of the Indians, and so forth. But not France, to my knowledge. All

PRIDE

the accidents of her history, by the mere fact that they happened in France, at once acquire a solemn and important air. It doesn't matter that the stages of the past contradict each other: the French admire them all with the same wholehearted enthusiasm.

Not only have they preserved stone monuments—Versailles, the Pantheon—but they have also kept alive the memories that go with them. Francis I, what a king! Scrupulous investigators describe his days and even his nights (see Lust) without sparing the least details. Well, and the century of Louis XIV? What luxury! What beauty! What elegance! But you wouldn't say that these qualities characterized the French Revolution of 1789? True, but how forceful the Assemblies, how eloquent Danton, how magnificent the integrity of Robespierre and the tenacity of Marat! And you certainly can't denigrate the heroism of the revolutionary troops battling their enemies drawn from every corner of Europe, lined up against them at Valmy. But they also fought against their own countrymen, in the Vendée.... Indeed they did—how extraordinary those peasants of the Vendée, fighting bravely for their principles!

See how Victor Hugo speaks of the Convention in *Ninety-Three*:

> We are approaching the great summit: the Convention.... On the physical globe we have the Himalaya mountains; in the world of history the Convention stands out. It is, perhaps, the culminating point of history.

Notice that he does not refer to the past of France—*all* of history finds its summit in this happening in Paris.

And Napoleon? This is a very special case. The Frenchman of today may be anything from a Communist to a Monarchist, but the Napoleonic myth touches the depths of his soul. You ought to hear, for example, the announcer of the *Son et lumière* at the Invalides speaking of the

PRIDE

Emperor. His voice seems to kneel before the titanic memory he has called up.

But the barricades of the Revolution of 1848, celebrated by Victor Hugo in *Les Misérables,* and the elegance of the Second Empire, are also important. And we hardly need discuss the First World War: all the towns of France that had a son in that contest are populated with more or less fitting monuments, in the shade of which mustachioed old men gather every Armistice Day to embrace and kiss each other tremblingly while the soldiers fall into formation. Juarès, the man who wouldn't go to war, and Clemenceau, the man who won it, are equally outstanding in this epic. And then the Second World War . . . and the Resistance, and in a short time we shall even see them speaking with admiration of General Pétain and the Vichy regime.

The last great hero is of course de Gaulle. Here is how a high school sophomore responded when the general's name appeared on a test: "De Gaulle saved Paris, opening the way for the allied landing in Normandy. He commanded the fleet and the air force from England." When de Gaulle died, Pompidou dedicated a phrase to him as beautiful as it was rhetorical: "France has been left a widow."

The French take pride in all their past and boast of it. Pierre Daninos, in his witty book *Les Carnets du Major W. Marmaduke Thompson,* draws attention to this indiscriminate admiration as a lapse in logic by the most logical people in the world, but to my way of thinking the logic of the French nation's ample reverence for their history is perfect. Today's liberal is proud of yesterday's Louis XIV, but that doesn't mean he wishes the return of absolute monarchy; someone who loves the liberty won by the Republic can continue to do so without giving up his fond memories of the times of glory. Put another way, the French want to save both what they had and what they have: the verb "to save" is very French (see Avarice).

Voltaire was a great cynic, the destroyer of religious and moral myths. Listen to him (*Tancred,* 1760) speaking of

PRIDE

France: *"A tous les coeurs bien nés, que la patrie est chère"* (How dear is the fatherland to every generous heart).

French patriotism shone brightly in the Second World War. Both sides committed themselves absolutely to the good of the country. Those who followed Charles Maurras, the collaborator, read his slogan every day in their paper: *La France, la France seule.* Those who preferred de Gaulle enthusiastically repeated his words: "France has lost a battle, but not the war. Let us unite to raise France up again." If the followers of de Gaulle accused those loyal to Pétain of selling out to Germany, Pétain's followers accused the others of selling out to England, and each group insisted that it represented the survival of what mattered most in all the world: the fatherland that both groups saw as capable of triumphing, though by different roads.

To understand how the French can take such pride in their economy, an area in which they do not especially excel, we have to remember that vanity is nearly always a function of what others possess. The richest man in a large family considers himself far superior to someone who has no close relatives to impress with his wealth. France is integrated into a grouping loosely called the Latin countries. The French have gotten a lot of mileage out of this denomination, and theirs is the idea (widely accepted, like everything else they think up) of extending the name Latin to the countries of Hispanic or Ibero America. By naming these countries after their grandfather rather than Spain and Portugal, their Iberian fathers, France brings them into a closer relationship with herself.

Of all the Latin countries, including both her immediate family in Europe and her more distant relatives in America, France is the richest, most advanced, and most powerful. From the time the Frenchman is a child, he sees Italian, Portuguese, and Spanish workmen all around him—people who have left their native country, where they couldn't make a living, and moved to fertile France, their adopted country, to find work and well-being. Never does

PRIDE

a French child hear that one of his own relatives has had to go to Málaga, Naples, or Coimbra and is sending back money at the end of the month to his family, left behind in Bordeaux or Lyon. The *bonne espagnole,* or Spanish maid, is so familiar in France that she has already passed into the folklore of the country with her errors in French. A typical joke:

> Madame: Put the cake *(gâteau)* in the Frigidaire.
> Maid: That's done, but he didn't want to go.
> Madame: What do you mean, he didn't want to go?
> Maid: The cat (Spanish *gato),* Madame; he tried to scratch me.
> Madame: Ha, ha! How stupid they are.

There is even a book published in France, *How To Deal with Spanish Maids.*

The syllogism would be simple even for a people less given to logic than the French: if workers from the other Latin countries come here to work, it is because we are the richest, the best, and the most powerful country in the group. (And if, in addition, Spanish republicans come here, as well as Rumanian, Hungarian, Polish, and Russian anti-Communists, it only shows that we are also the freest people in the world. Have we forgotten anyone else?)

De Gaulle spoke of a Europe stretching from the Atlantic to the Urals, in which France would play the dominant role. He was simply repeating a centuries-old thesis. Whenever France has failed to decide the fate of Europe by the force of arms (for example, Louis XIV or Napoleon), she has tried to achieve preponderance by cultural or social means. Napoleon was overthrown by a coalition of kings, but he had already sown the seeds of a new French product, revolution, that ended by destroying the monarchies that conquered him on the field of battle. The national Revolutions of 1848 which shook all Europe were, at bottom, a form of revenge for Waterloo.

It would have seemed very natural to the French that a

supranational European institution like the Catholic Church should have had its seat in Paris. Since this hasn't been the case, France has always maintained an ambivalent attitude toward the papacy. She stayed at its side after the Reformation, but only in the posture of a new interpretation. Her doctrine of Gallicanism was chiefly calculated to demonstrate independence—the national church of France needed no lessons from Rome. And when Napoleon tried to maintain the tradition of Charlemagne and Charles V by having the legendary power of the pontificate crown him Emperor, he added two very French touches. First, the Pope came to Paris; Napoleon did not go to Rome, as was traditional. Second, at the solemn moment Pius VII was preparing to place the crown on his head, Napoleon took it from him and crowned himself, and then crowned Josephine in turn. It wasn't personal pride that moved him, though this fault was not lacking in the makeup of the little Corsican. It was the national pride of France.

Whenever the country has returned to the fold, it has always been as the favorite sheep—"the preferred daughter of the Church"—or else in a stance of heterodoxy, formal if not substantial. France has given us the worker priests who scandalize so many of the faithful, and through the voice of her bishops she has taken an attitude of patient understanding toward the papal bull *Humanae Vitae.* Currently, of course, the great projects of Catholic reform are Dutch and German, not French. France's support for them is only lukewarm, because whatever she doesn't invent herself never seems very important to her.

France is the only country in the West to have attempted to substitute a national calendar for the Gregorian calendar which the rest of us use. The new names imposed during the French Revolution—Thermidor, Vendémiaire, Brumaire, etc.—didn't prosper, but the attempt is symbolic. France is proud of her Roman past, but the great popular hero among French children today is Asterix the Gaul.

PRIDE

When a Frenchman travels, he almost never speaks any language but his own—that idiom which all civilized persons *ought* to know. And he never finds it natural to observe other people's customs, either.

In his book *L'Antiguide,* Pierre Daninos mentions the reaction of a Frenchwoman who owned an apartment in Laredo, on the Cantabrian coast, when an interviewer for Paris television asked her about the problems of adjusting to the Spanish way of life. "Imagine!" she said indignantly. "We are the ones expected to adjust to their mealtime hours."

With history supporting them, a geography of incredibly beautiful landscapes, a city completely fascinating from every point of view as their capital, a culture praised by themselves even beyond its true and very considerable merit, and with a Monsieur or Madame placed before even the humblest of surnames, the citizens of France are psychologically prepared to face the challenges of each new day, not to mention a run-of-the-mill tourist.

In every country the tourist is a guest, but a guest who pays, and that should give him certain rights. The fundamental problem in the relations between the Frenchman and the tourist is that the former believes he is living in an earthly paradise, into which he has generously admitted the latter, more often than not his intellectual and cultural inferior. It is revealing of French thinking on this subject that, when a Frenchman wants to show his hostility to a foreigner, he calls him *métèque.* The *métèques,* remember, were foreigners—uncultivated and barbaric— who lived among the refined Greeks. Assuming that today's Frenchmen are the true Athenians of our time, any poor wretch who is attracted by their light and goes to their country should naturally aspire to nothing more than to look and pay for doing so. Certainly in no circumstances may he attempt to exercise any right on the frivolous pretext that traveling and visiting cost him much more in France than they would in other parts of Europe or Asia. Such a comparison is simply absurd.

PRIDE

Statistically, this situation shows up in a decline in the number of days that the average tourist spends in France, particularly in Paris. The figures are impressive enough to have given serious concern to the French government in recent years. On the level of anecdote, the experiences of the ordinary traveler in France will bear witness to the same phenomenon. At one hotel, a traveler who arrives at 4:00 A.M. may be told that "this is no hour to be going to bed" and on those grounds be denied a room (this happened to my nephew). In another hotel, at the opposite end of the country, the rooms may be freezing. When the prospective guest protests, the owner replies, "What do you expect? That I am going to spend my money keeping the room warm just in case you should decide to come today?" (This happened to me.)

I have been visiting France for many years now. Not *once* have I ever found a deficiency in the service of a hotel or a restaurant smoothed over with an apology or excuse. The Frenchman simply can't believe that anyone sufficiently favored by destiny to have arrived in his fabulous land could permit himself the luxury of arguing about its prices or conveniences.

These latter, everyone knows, often shine by their absence. One luxury hotel has a beautiful marble courtyard with fountains. To get to one's rooms, one journeys along an interminable narrow corridor, and the rooms themselves prove to be decorated with the stylistic grace of fifty years ago. The hotel owners haven't attempted to capture a fashionable mood of Art Nouveau; they simply haven't ever changed their draperies, their lamps—direct descendants of Quinquet gas-burners—or their tubs, which are so unbelievably high that one almost needs to jump up to get into them.

The particular room I'm referring to had armoires in the corners of the room next to a mansard window. To put a suit or overcoat in them, one had to creep in as if into a cave, and the lamp always tipped over because the cord passed precisely in front of the door.

In the more modest hotels, one finds the same superan-

PRIDE

nuation, but not the tub. When they have tried to modernize, they have divided their rooms in two and put in showers almost on top of the narrow beds.

In Paris (these facts have been reported officially) not a single hotel was built between 1935 and 1955. From 1955 to 1967, the years of the most intense tourism the world has ever known, five hotels were constructed, two of them super deluxe. Many times I have pointed out this shortcoming to Frenchmen, but never have they apologized for it.

As for sanitary problems, one must remember that the Frenchman does not understand the complaints of foreigners very well, mainly because the majority of French houses, and particularly the houses of Paris, lack the most elementary hygienic facilities. It just seems absurd to him that a foreigner should place such emphasis on what he hardly misses. A chief source of French hostility toward Americans is the fact that they are always griping about the lack of hot water in France; these Sybaritic requirements, contrasting so sharply with the Americans' over-all cultural barbarism, are one more cause for the resentment that the French already harbor on other grounds against their allies from across the Atlantic.

Obviously, many different elements enter into French distrust of Americans. Leftists, because they prefer the U.S.S.R. or China, hate the Yankees; rightists, because they are irritated as nationalists that the United States had to aid France in two wars and later saved her from ruin by the Marshall Plan, also despise them. The average Frenchman shares the resentment of both groups, and it was one of de Gaulle's master strokes that he was able to echo these vague feelings and apply them in his isolationist policies of abandoning NATO and attempting to place the franc in a position of strength superior to the dollar. (De Gaulle—as I intimated before—achieved many triumphs simply by saying out loud what the average Frenchman didn't dare say for fear of seeming out of date.)

Since the world is a complicated place, the will to win

PRIDE

sometimes isn't enough (Czechoslovakia on the one hand, the events of May 1968 in France, on the other, and the devaluation of the franc in 1969 have shown that the policy of isolationism may have had more spirit than substance), but the impulse doesn't therefore disappear: in the usual French fashion, it just recedes for a while as a matter of convenience.

In the summer of 1968, while I was eating supper in an outdoor café in the rue Saint-Benoit, I fell into conversation with a young couple. They had taken their vacation in Spain, and it was obvious that, if the sun, the beaches, and especially the prices had pleased them (see Avarice), everything else had struck them as absolutely second-rate.

"Look," the young man finished, "I've traveled in many parts of Europe and I've reached the conclusion that the only place where tourists are well treated is France."

After I recovered from my shock, I told him that he didn't even read his own newspapers, or he would have known that the French government was concerned because fewer and fewer tourists were coming to France; that the hotels were full—there being so few of them—at certain times of the year, but empty the rest; that it had been necessary to promise French taxi drivers "courtesy coupons" so that they would be friendlier to foreigners; and that prices were climbing higher and higher. Finally, I drew his attention to what we ourselves were going to have to pay in the modest restaurant where we were sitting.

Had the incident occurred today, I could have mentioned quite a few concrete facts. In 1969, for example, there were fewer tourists in France than in 1967, and they also spent less because they stayed for a shorter time. The average American spent the equivalent of 1,210 francs in Italy, 1,160 in Great Britain, 1,120 in Spain, and only 871 in France. Of the millions spent abroad by Germans, France captured only 21 per cent despite its geographic proximity (*L'Express,* February 2, 1970).

PRIDE

More than half of all French hotels date back to the nineteenth century. Only 15 per cent were constructed between 1945 and 1967, compared with 70 per cent in the United States and 80 per cent in Spain. French hotels had twenty-five bathrooms for every hundred rooms; Swiss hotels had thirty-two, Italian hotels forty-seven. The ratio of prices in 1967 for the same sort of lodgings was one hundred in France, eighty-one in Italy, and forty-five in Spain (*L'Express,* October 12, 1970).

I'm not sure whether this new evidence would have impressed my friend any more than the conditions I was able to cite on the spot. In any case, his answer was characteristically French. "Well, good, perhaps so. But," he said, motioning with his hand toward the scene around us, "a street like the rue Saint-Benoit doesn't exist anywhere else in the world."

The funny thing is, if he had said this in front of Notre Dame, the Place des Vosges, or any of a thousand other marvels in Paris, he would have been completely right. The rue Saint-Benoit, however, is decorated in summer with a ridiculous array of stars and circles of light bulbs, quite worthy of a holiday celebration in the tiniest Spanish town. No matter. In his opinion, France was the best of all countries, so it followed that this street was the finest that anyone could possibly imagine.

That particular Frenchman, like all the others I know, including the most intelligent and cultured among them, resented the criticism of foreigners as if it were absolutely stupid. The attitude of the French toward the traveler is tinged with sympathy only when the traveler falls all over himself with admiration for what he sees, and overlooks any defects he may encounter. This may help explain the position in Paris of foreign students, toward whom everyone feels so protective and friendly. The French think it's fine that students come from every corner of the world to study in the center of all intellectual life; for one thing, they know that the students will later become France's most enthusiastic boosters. The toughest concierge feels kindly toward students and even lets them go up to the apartments in her building to ask for old paper to sell (one of their stratagems for survival), and waiters allow them to sit at a café table for hours and hours with only an orange crush or a glass of beer. The hardness of the French toward foreigners disappears in this case along with their avarice in a curious and—why not admit it?—extremely attractive manner.

The freedom to dress exactly as one pleases in Paris is a good thing for a young man without any money. No matter what he wears, it's hard for him to attract any attention, so his budget is freed from a common strain. As a matter of fact, a person can live very well in Paris today if he is completely down-and-out or exceptionally rich. Only the man who thinks of himself as middle class and doesn't dare take off his tie runs into difficulties, economic and social.

A taste for pomp, uniforms, and brilliant ceremonies is typically French. When the revolution put an end to palace ceremonies, so-called ceremonies of the people took their place, and the Convention commissioned the painter David to produce great tableaux in which he put the sacred mountains of the fatherland, processions of virgins and children, veterans, and liberty trees. In some of these festivities, hymns written especially for the occasion were sung and doves were released; in other convocations, solemn oaths were pronounced while cannons rumbled and thundered. Napoleon gave eagles and victorious commemorations to the French, and the regimes that followed him continued the tradition. The bourgeois king Louis Philippe was the only exception. "His example," remarks a historian, "shows that unpretentious courts are doomed to failure, for they disappoint, at one and the same time, both the pride and the imagination of the French."

As a matter of fact, with each successive regime the show has gone on. The Cuirassiers of the Republic, with their metal helmets and plumes, have no reason to envy the retinue of any absolute monarch; when they form two ranks in the Opéra with their sabers unsheathed (the graceful French expression for this is *sable au clair,* "saber in the light"), they impress everyone who sees them.

De Gaulle was yet another incarnation of the dream so many share. *Le Grande Charles* did not overlook the slightest detail of protocol, as those who tried to minimize it knew only too well. The *chansonniers,* or singing lampoon artists, cracked joke after joke about his lofty and majestic bearing. The French people enjoyed these witticisms, but in their hearts they loved the ceremony with which their chief of state surrounded himself. De Gaulle is gone now, but the dream he embodied lives on. No matter how sophisticated and skeptical the French think they are, the Arc de Triomphe at the end of the Champs-Elysées, with its reminders of Napoleon and its eternal flame flickering in memory of those who died in battle, remains a thing of great seriousness to every one of them.

Yes. The Frenchman is ironic, witty, and skeptical, capable, like Voltaire, of destroying or at least deflating with a *mot d'esprit* many kinds of rhetoric. But let the subject turn to his national history, and he becomes solemn and respectful. Napoleon, for example, might be analyzed with equally rigorous scholarship in his capacity as a husband cuckolded by Josephine or in his role of victor in great battles. Nonetheless, when these battles are commemorated, the spectators do not remember the *cocu.* Everyone's attention is riveted to the memory of the triumphant general.

In the issue of *Le Figaro* for December 2, 1968, an article recounted the ceremony of commissioning the cadets of the Saint-Cyr military college. The headline itself was rather revealing: "For the commemoration of the Battle of Austerlitz, only the sun failed to show up." The reporter went on to describe, in minute and respectful detail, the historical re-enactment of the battle, in which some cadets played the Austrians and others the troops of the Emperor, with the expected result. Before this brilliantly col-

PRIDE

orful pageant began, the chronicle continued, the new Saint-Cyriens knelt to receive their *casoar* plumes and white gloves from the graduates of the class that had preceded them. "For them it corresponded to the conferring of knighthood. No veteran could remain indifferent to this rite that marked their entrance into the military estate."

Here we have a group of republicans in the year 1968 taking part in a ceremony to commemorate a battle won by Napoleon in his dream of conquering Europe. The internal strength that keeps France on its feet, despite wars more or less lost and economic crises more or less overcome, is this total acceptance of a glorious past and the solidarity with it felt by every Frenchman, no matter how greatly ideas have changed, no matter how different the current political regime may be.

"One always expects a Frenchman to be the opposite of a provincial, that is, that he be sure of himself." So says Roger Vailland in his book *Le Regard froid,* and it is an impression shared by all the foreigners who come to Paris. Not only are Parisians confident and at ease in every situation, they make sure that no one else is.

INDIVIDUAL PRIDE

French national pride is justified—assuming pride can ever be justified at all—by a brilliant history and a remarkably beautiful geography. But what about the personal pride of the individual Frenchman?

Individual pride was born with the French Revolution. This revolution was the most intelligent of all in that it did not attempt to create equality but something perhaps more important to mankind: the feeling of being equal.

On my first visit to France, coming from a Spain that was divided and exhausted from its Civil War, I noted

PRIDE

something extremely important. When the forces of the Right sang "their" hymn in the Assembly, they sang the Marseillaise; when the forces of the Left sang "their" hymn, they sang the Marseillaise also. After a difficult and violent session, the deputies on the conservative benches would sometimes intone, or rather shout out, the national anthem, to show their patriotism. Not wanting to join in with them, the deputies on the Left would listen in silence, but when the rightists finished, they raised in turn the cry of the oppressed of the world. It was, again, the Marseillaise, chosen over the Internationale even by the Communists. I thought then that despite the profound division of ideas in France, it would be difficult for the country to suffer a civil war, because people can't fight from opposite trenches with the same music and words on their lips. As the event proved, not even the trauma of Algeria carried the French to fratricide.

The French Revolution gave the people something more. It gave them the slogan "Liberty, Equality, Fraternity," now emblazoned on every public building. It gave them the impression, which, I repeat, to my way of thinking is more important than the reality, that they were free and equal men.

But the most important contribution of the revolution toward building up the egos of the French was its concession of titles to everyone. Other revolutions have tended to lower everyone to the same rank, to tug on the upper classes, in other words, until they tumble to the level of the rest. The *señor* and *señora* are converted into *compañero* and *camarada,* the Russian *Gospodin* becomes *Tovarishch,* the *Herr* becomes *Kamerad.* The French Revolution, however, as the result of a long historical process involving the chopping off of heads and the arbitration of Napoleon, did not support the original, infantile aspiration of some that the poor *sans-culottes* should rule. On the contrary—and this is what has kept it alive in the hearts of the French—it gave every French citizen the title *Monsieur* or *Madame,* until then reserved for a select elite.

PRIDE

These titles were an important gift and accounted for the self-confidence that spread to every social class in a way not seen in other Latin countries. Miguel Mihura, with his extraordinary sense of observation, took note of the phenomenon in his play *Ninette y un señor de Murcia*. In one scene a Spanish refugee in Paris appears on stage and explains the change in status she experienced by crossing the border. Her profession remained the same—she hawked green vegetables. But whereas in Spain she was known as "the woman of the green grocery," in Paris she had been metamorphosed into Madame Sánchez and she could even wear a hat, something that was prohibited to her social class in Madrid.

Not only is it impossible for a foreigner to address anyone in France without first saying Madame or Monsieur; the fact is, the French themselves enjoy these titles and revel in saying them at every opportunity, as if they were something new. The owner of a modest hotel where I stayed a few days in Font-Romeu, in the eastern Pyrenees, told me about a conversation she had had with a neighbor:

"And then Mme. Paulet said to me, 'But Mme. Dupont, don't you think that this matter can be arranged?'

"And I answered, 'Ay, Mme. Paulet, I think it will be very difficult.'

"And she said, 'But Mme. Dupont, if they were to make an effort . . .'

"To which I replied, 'Mme. Paulet, don't count on it.'"

Her description of the dialogue went on for ten minutes. Not once did she allude to the persons who had taken part in it without specifying (by the title Madame) that they were ladies.

Where the usage of the word Madame seems most striking of all to the visitor from Spain is in the world of doormen and porters, who are most often women. "Doorwoman" *(portera)* in Spanish has unjustly acquired unpleasant associations: we say that "she shouts like a doorwoman" or "she's nothing but a doorwoman." In France, the concierge is much more important, thanks to revolutionary statutes that looked to her as a natural ally against the aristocrats. Napoleon's prefects kept her on in the role of auxiliary to the public authorities and today Madame la Concierge exercises a very obvious power over the neighbors, who need her even to prove that they are alive, since she is the one charged by the law with testifying about it.

The respected title of Monsieur or Madame is extended to persons of every social class and, most significantly of all, to politicians and criminals. Accustomed as I am to the diatribes and disdain that Spanish newspapers heap on their political enemies, it has always filled me with admiration to find right-wing papers in France referring to Stalin as M. Stalin and to Khrushchev as M. Khrushchev. And more amazing still, *L'Humanité* speaking of its capitalist enemy as M. Nixon.

Not even hardened malefactors get slighted in the matter of titles. A murderer will be characterized as a gentleman every time he is referred to and, for the judge, the use of *vous,* the formal form of the pronoun "you," is obligatory whether he is addressing the worst of criminals or the humblest beggar accused of robbery.

In 1793 there were revolutionary attempts to use the informal pronoun *tu* and to call everyone *citoyen,* but this quickly faded away. Frenchmen today use *vous* to address everyone, and in old-fashioned families they even manage to maintain this level of formality between man and wife. In *Bonjour, Tristesse,* when the heroine is present, the mistress of her father addresses him as *vous,* even though the girl knows their relationship.

In recent years many French businesses have tried to adopt American business methods, and now a few firms have instituted the sort of human relations between bosses and employees that they observed on the other side of the Atlantic. The magazine *Elle* questioned a number of employees about the new program, with mixed results. In general, fifty-year-old secretaries who had been with their companies a long time thought it was monstrous to be expected to address the president and general director as "Albert," while some of the younger secretaries felt that it was only natural. Later a reporter questioned some of the husbands of these women and found that the great majority regarded the new "fraternization" between their wives and their wives' bosses as "disagreeable and pointless," while 35 per cent went further and called it "dangerous." "When I imagine my wife calling the director by his first name and he answering her as Jacqueline," one of the men remarked, "it strikes me as slightly indecent. It's a bit like standing in one's underwear in front of a stranger—which is essentially what the director is, after working hours are over. I have the recurring fantasy that from nine to twelve and from two to six my wife is showing herself in her underthings to a character she hardly knows and I've never met."

The pronoun *vous* defines, limits, and maintains social distance. It is an attempt to remain aloof rather than a sign of respect; its use results from the egocentricity of the French, who do not wish to be bothered. And the usage survives despite all revolutionary shocks. A Spanish journalist who happened to be in Paris during the events of May 1968 described the revolution to me partly by comparing it to our own of 1936, and in so doing mentioned that he had heard students addressing people as "comrade" instead of "Monsieur." I asked him, "But did they use the familiar or formal form of the verb?" *"Vous." "Comrade* and *vous?"* Then don't worry. They are completely embedded in a centuries-old tradition and they find it easier to yank up street paving stones than an idiom.

And besides, if they ever did suppress the form, they would eliminate a delightful embellishment of physical love. "To use the familiar pronoun *tu,* you have to sleep together first," advises a French proverb. And even then. . . . Madame de Rênal and Julien Sorel are speaking to each other in bed following their first encounter:

PRIDE

> He: Would you regret losing your life?
> She: Ah! Very much at this moment, but I would not regret having known you.

Vous is used by both characters. (*The Red and the Black*, Book I, Chapter 16.)

POLITENESS

In September 1909 a ministerial circular notified French civil servants that good manners were obligatory in their dealings with the public. A cartoon by Forain in *Le Figaro* on October 4 commented on this development. In it a typical bourgeois couple is seen shrinking back in terror as a functionary towers over them, apparently ready to strike them down. The caption reads: "Permit me to suggest that you be so very good as to direct your request to another window" *(Je vous ai déjà prié d'avoir l'extrême obligeance de vous adresser à un autre guichet).*

The joke in 1909 was the contrast between the courteous words and the hostile gesture, and it still is today because the French very commonly wrap the most ordinary of statements in the trappings of politeness (which sometimes seem extremely beautiful in their language). A letter that concludes with a phrase as baroque as *"Veuillez agréer, Monsieur, l'assurance de mes sentiments les plus dévoués"* may be written with venom. The same custom prevails in daily conversation. With a Monsieur or a Madame as his opening, the proud Frenchman can go on to make his compatriot or a stranger feel the deepest humiliation.

> I even witnessed a noisy fight between two women who came to blows without completely abandoning courtesy.
> "Oh, Madame!" shouted one, giving the other a good scratching.

PRIDE

"Oh, Mademoiselle!" shouted the other, replying with a lusty pulling of hair.

A. Palacio Valdés, *La guerra injusta*, 1917.

Ah, non! This is a key expression in France, one that is used with tremendous emphasis in situations where in other countries a simple "I don't think so" or "Probably not" would suffice. Questions as normal as whether a house has heating or if a bus passes through the neighborhood elicit the answer *ah, non!* and the phrase tends to be violent and definitive. It is almost always accompanied by a shake of the head from left to right and a little upward. It is sometimes varied with a Monsieur or Madame—*Ah, non, Monsieur!*—but this doesn't take off its edge; on the contrary, it seems to make the matter worse. The Monsieur isn't meant to insinuate that you didn't know what you were asking; rather, it seems to show that the question was even more absurd in that it was posed by a gentleman who ought to be better informed.

Rudeness can also begin with "I beg your pardon!" or *"Pardon, Monsieur! Je vous en prie!"* Formulas like these in other countries are the equivalent of a declaration of friendship, or at least of surrender, but not in France. The *Pardon, Monsieur* or the *Je vous demande pardon* may be followed by an overwhelming verbal offensive, complete with florid rhetorical flourishes lasting for hours.

Because not for nothing is France known as the country of elegant speech and reason. The French can discuss anything for hours, and so long as there are arguments to present, they enjoy the game. A friend of mine, a diplomat, used to touch off this mechanism, hidden in every Frenchman, with a simple trick. He would merely arrive at the movies when the lights were on and sit down without the assistance of the usher, who in France is almost always a woman and someone you tip with a few small coins. The usher could be counted on to hurry over and ask my friend for his ticket. Tearing it, she would remind him, "And the tip, Monsieur?" "What tip?" he would ask. "I sat down by

PRIDE

myself. You didn't perform any service for me, so why should I have to pay you for something you didn't do?"

The usher would insist, and in a minute everyone in the surrounding seats would be divided into one of two groups: those who believed that my friend was quite right not to pay for what he never received, and those who argued the opposite, that the usher counted on the tip as part of her income and so it was her due, whether she actually performed any service or not. Generally this second group was more numerous because the recalcitrant was a foreigner and the French become irritated when any outsider attempts to change the laws—perfect though unwritten—of French society. The scene usually concluded with the arrival of the manager, who always had to decide that the customer was right, since as a matter of fact, despite all appearances, the tip is not obligatory. A curious commentary on all this once came to my attention in a tourist brochure about Paris, which stated: "Tipping is not obligatory, but it is a deeply rooted custom which must be observed."

> The manners and customs that people treat carelessly as matters of no importance are sometimes what cause others to judge us favorably or unfavorably.
>
> La Bruyère, *Les Caractères,* 1688.

The Frenchman's love for glorious gestures has passed into history; the *beau geste* (title of the novel about the Foreign Legion which made us dream as adolescents) perfumes the memory of its past. "Form a group around the white plumes of my helmet!" said Henry IV. This is how the cult of Bayard was born, Bayard the knight without fear or fault. And later the cult of Cyrano de Bergerac, valiant, sentimental, and ugly.

One of the famous phrases of French history underlined a *beau geste.* The scene, the battle of Fontenoy; face to face, the troops of England and France, momentarily still

PRIDE

before the commencement of battle. Out stepped the French general, resplendent in collar and cuffs of lace and wearing a plumed hat: "Messieurs the English: be the first to open fire."

Exquisite. So very exquisite, in fact, that skeptics have sought to discover a hidden motive. According to one interpretation, the French general invited the English to fire first not merely because the gesture was elegant, but because cold calculation recommended the move. Loading a musket in those days was difficult and time-consuming; at the distance separating the two armies, acting first constituted a disadvantage rather than an advantage, since the enemy could advance while you reloaded, and mow you down at short range before you had a chance to get off a second round.

Ah, historians are sometimes so very disappointing....

SELFISHNESS

Pride produces friction among humans, because one who imagines himself to occupy an exalted station expects that everyone will give way before him. But in France, reason has so much influence on people's minds that, at the last moment, when a fight is about to start, they manage to hold their tempers. Proud himself, the Frenchman is able to understand that others have a sense of pride as well, and this lessens the severity of everyday conversations. Shops in Paris, for example, close and open whenever they feel like it; the shopkeeper admits no responsibility whatever to his clientele and if it is convenient for him to open at eleven in the morning, that is what he does. In any other country in the world this would touch off a protest from the would-be customer, who feels bound by an unwritten contract with the shopkeeper. The shopkeeper, in turn—it is supposed in other latitudes—is

PRIDE

obligated to keep his establishment open at certain hours so that I or anyone else can shop at that time. It's a matter of public service, and the public has its rights.

This line of reasoning is nonsensical in Paris. The last time I stayed in the capital I complained several times about the frivolousness of the commercial establishments near the "Coupole." Some posted announcements that they opened at noon, others didn't even bother to put up a sign: whoever wanted to could try later, the others *tant pis.* The tremendous avarice of the French, about which we shall speak later, shines by its absence whenever a storekeeper wants to be somewhere else. So naturally I found no sympathy at all for my complaints. Aside from the principle pointed out before which holds that a foreigner is never right when he contests a custom of the French, everyone understood the shopkeepers perfectly. To open when one feels like it, *c'est la liberté, Monsieur.*

Another symptom of French egotism is their system of highways. Thirty years ago French highways were the best in Europe. Today they are the worst, not because of their surface, which is well cared for, but because of their layout. Just notice some time what happens to most of them when they come to a major city. In countries conscious of tourism, urban centers are avoided; the highway circles the city so that the tourist may proceed directly to his destination. Not in France. In France every visiting motorist has probably suffered the same anguished, sinking sensation at the sight of a roadsign proclaiming CENTRE VILLE ET TOUTES DIRECTIONS, which means that the flood of automobiles on the highway has got to penetrate the narrow streets of an ancient French city, mingle and jostle with all the cars moving about on local errands, and then edge away again, with great difficulty, toward the other side of town, where the motorists will find the hoped-for sign "To Paris" or "To Lyon" or "To the Belgian frontier." This doesn't happen in Italy or Spain, but in France, of course, it is absolutely logical. The French make their highways for themselves and they go to their provincial cities for business or pleasure. They see no reason to change their customs so that a few foreigners can travel about more conveniently.

Nationalism is much more important than the French will admit. We should not forget that the French term *chauvinisme* has passed into every language. When I read André Gide's *Return from the USSR* years ago, I noticed this chauvinism strongly present. The writer had gone to Russia with high hopes and had come back disillusioned, but one got the impression that what annoyed him most of all, more than any particular feature of the proletarian conquests, was the proud Soviet belief that they were the first in everything. A revealing page recounts his irritation when the Soviets showed him things as simple as a kindergarten or a tractor factory and then said immediately, "You people in France haven't got anything like this, have you?" It was enough to turn him into an enemy of the new regime, and to cause the regime in retaliation to ban his works in the U.S.S.R.

PRIDE OF LANGUAGE

"One Hundred and Fifty Million French Speakers Assembled at Versailles Want the Heavens to Use French." Reason is not always displayed at its best in the titles of French magazine articles, but this one from *Paris-Match* (October 1968) is less of an exaggeration than it sounds. It refers to the decision adopted by the delegates of thirty-two French-speaking countries to launch a communications satellite for the sole purpose of serving as a link between the cultures that accept Paris as their guiding star.

French is the official language of France, Belgium, Senegal, Guinea, Mali, Nigeria, Chad, Gabon, the Republic of the Congo, Ivory Coast, Burundi, Volta, Togo, Dahomey,

PRIDE

Cameroon, and Haiti. It is one of two or more official languages in Switzerland, Rwanda, Madagascar, North Vietnam, South Vietnam, Laos, Cambodia, and Mauritania. It is used extensively in Canada, Algeria, Mauritius, and Morocco.

The cultural pride of the French derives in large measure from their love for their language, a language that is soft, rich, and velvety, perfectly adapted for use in any routine or extraordinary situation and always poetic. It is a national treasure, one that deserves to be pampered and carefully tended, which is exactly what everyone does to the limits of his ability. A desk attendant in a hotel, a cop on his beat, or a waiter (no need to mention the maître d') in a restaurant will explain the simplest things to you in the clearest, most definitive form possible. They all choose their words with unusual subtlety in order to express their thoughts with the greatest elegance possible. The French believe that their language is divine, and one of the grievances they have against foreigners is the way they mistreat it. With Americans in particular the French have no patience at all; contrary to the fond belief of the misguided gringo, his attempt to speak the language of the country he is visiting, rather than being appreciated, is received by the French as a personal affront. As he slowly sounds his mispronounced words one by one, the listening Frenchman's expression is a marvelous study. Now and then he closes his eyes, like someone who has taken a blow.

This is also the reason why French lecturers are unique. English lecturers stutter; Italians and Spaniards give discourses; but the French lecture in a generally even tone, avoiding ups and downs but giving each word and sentence its precise shading, as if they were professional engravers. So great is the style of French speakers that they often manage—as their playwrights do also—to pass off a series of harmless commonplaces for the epitome of interest. I remember once when Georges Duhamel visited Madrid; he spoke about famous Frenchmen and included all the foreigners who had ever triumphed in Paris, from

Picasso to the Rumanian actress Lupescu, taking in the Armenian Aznavour along the way. The Spanish writer who accompanied me at the lecture did not share my enthusiasm as we left. "In sum," he concluded, "a telephone book." "And doesn't it amaze you," I replied, "that he helped us pass a delightful hour by reciting a list of names?"

On a lesser plane, the great achievement of the French is the art of conversation. *"Une heure de conversation vaut mieux que cinquante livres,"* wrote Madame de Sévigné in 1649, and in fact conversation has been valued so highly in France that the associated concepts of the *mot d'esprit* and the *homme d'esprit* have passed to other countries. To have *esprit*—that is, a rapid wit, or speed and profundity in one's rejoinders—is considered more important than how one looks. *"Les personnes d'esprit ne sont jamais laides,"* said Piron in *La Métromanie* in 1738—people with wit are never homely. People with poor taste, a corollary goes, turn out badly: *"Le mauvais goût mène au crime,"* was the opinion of Sainte-Beuve in 1866.

As surely as at any time in the past, anyone today who has the ability to say clever things will achieve immortality, while another man may write three volumes of important prose and be forgotten. Actually, of course, the people who launch witty remarks tend to be the very writers who turn out the volumes of prose. Voltaire, better known for his epigrams than for his fat encyclopedic texts, is a classic case, and shows the importance of neat phrases in the culture of France. When François Mauriac met Mr. and Mrs. Daniel Rops, he made rich and famous by his studies of the Bible and she decked out in a marvelous mink coat, the novelist was unable to suppress a comment that all Paris would be repeating the next day. Gently caressing the fur of her coat, he sighed with a tender, nostalgic look, *"Ah, ce doux Jésus . . ."*—Ah, Jesus is sweet.

The Frenchman's sense of superiority vis-à-vis his neighbors is reinforced every time he finds that something he regards as genuinely important really is better at home than abroad. No one can deny, for example, that the Germans and the English are good businessmen, practical, and perhaps better than the French in industrial technology—but what a lack of style!

"*Esprit* and genius lose 25 per cent of their value when they land in England," remarks Julien Sorel in *The Red and the Black* (Book II, Chapter 7). Elsewhere in the same novel, the Marquis de La Mole reminds the protagonist that the citizens of Hamburg had to gather in groups of four to grasp the sense of a *bon mot* or clever phrase. Voltaire took a general view of the situation: "Someone had to teach Hurón, but the job looked hard to the Abbot of St. Ives because he assumed that a man not born in France would necessarily lack common sense." (*L'Ingenu*, Chapter 20.)

The French regard their language as a common patrimony and to offend it is to offend them all. No social class has escaped this national obsession; the Communist Duclos pays as much attention to the elegance of his discourses as the Gaullist Couve de Murville. *L'Humanité*, far to the Left, carries a regular column answering questions from readers about the proper pronunciation of doubtful words. One can hardly imagine a Communist paper in Spain or the United States using so much space for problems of linguistic style.

Delight in the language is universal: not even the poor are an exception. A Spanish beggar as likely as not will cry out simply "Alms for the love of God" or "Will anyone give to one who has nothing?" but a beggar in France is apt to write some comment on the sidewalk like the one I saw last summer in Montparnasse: *"Je n'aime pas faire ça, mais maintenant je n'ai pas de la chance"* (I don't like doing this, but at the moment I'm down on my luck). The most stupefying aspect of this petition was that its writer was a dwarf with a long beard seated in a wheelchair, which augmented the poignancy of his expression "at the moment."

PRIDE

The Frenchman's love for brilliant phrases is in constant opposition to his faculty for reasoned and logical criticism, which carries with it a certain coldness. The resulting tension can be seen in Jean Cocteau's reply when asked who was the most important poet in French history.

"Victor Hugo, alas," he answered sadly. Because even though Cocteau's culture and esthetics forced him to regard Hugo as hackneyed and out of date, in his heart the older poet still reigned supreme because of the force of his language and the brilliance of his images. He holds the same place in the hearts of nearly all the French. Let us not forget that in France, much to her credit, the elite and the masses do not follow different or even contradictory paths, as in other countries. Authors who are admired by the most demanding critics sell thousands and thousands of copies.

The play of words is constant and in the last analysis untranslatable: *"Il y avait trop de beau monde pour que ce fut aussi du monde beau."* (Françoise Giroud, *L'Express,* September 9–15, 1968.)

The 1968 disturbances in Paris have already been mentioned as well as the inscriptions on the walls of the Sorbonne, the Odeón theater, and the buildings along nearby streets. The young people of France, intoxicated with liberty, threw themselves into the task of saying everything and saying it well. Many sentences have found their way into literary collections, despite the anonymity of their authors. The underlying anarchism of some of the phrases served only to add zest, so to speak, to their literary pirouettes. "It's not a question of organizing or understanding, but of living" (cited in *Le Monde,* May 25, 1968). "I take my wishes for realities because I believe in the reality of my wishes" (written on the Sorbonne, May 30). "Be realistic, ask the impossible" (written on several walls of the Sorbonne during the revolution).

The young Frenchmen were sustained by their enthusiasm by hours of discussion. In the United States a similar revolution would have evolved into a pot festival or a riot; in Spain, the sacking of churches; but in Paris the young were satisfied to talk and talk. Perhaps their favorite sport, reasoning, has a practical use—revolution.

"Those who work get bored when they stop. Those who never work are never bored" (a Sorbonne wall, May 17, 1968). Thoughts for the sake of thought, meant to stimulate the intelligence. "The revolution is also fighting for beauty. Help us drive ugliness out of the world" (Sorbonne), or, "We refuse to live in a world where the certainty that we shall not die of hunger is purchased at the cost of exposing ourselves to the danger of dying of boredom" (Cohn-Bendit in *Le Monde,* May 14, 1968).

Jean-Paul Sartre addressed them, saying: "You have a limited amount of imagination like everyone else, but you have more ideas than your elders."

Writing French well is indispensable; a letter that merely discloses one's passionate feelings is not enough. "Your first declaration of love," observed a popular French woman writer, "made me weep with laughter. Oh, seducers with bad grammar! Refrain from writing the woman of your thoughts, especially if she appreciates beautiful language. You risk losing whatever chances you had." (Maud Secquard de Belleroche, *L'Ordinatrice,* 1948.)

No wonder so many French idioms and phrases have established themselves as permanent guests in other languages—they define things precisely without any loss of elegance. In German, in Spanish, or in English, one may say today, *"La beauté du geste, le physique du rôle."* One mentions *joie de vivre* when one is happy, or *déjà vu* when one is suddenly gripped by the feeling—well studied by the psychologists—that something is new yet familiar at the same time. Someone we admire has *savoir-faire,* a woman has *chic.* The American astronauts begin their long trips back from the moon with a *rendezvous* with the command module.

Some languages even use French expressions for situations which in France are described in some other way. In the United States, for example, *faux pas* describes what the French themselves call a *gaffe*.

After a long while, even a Frenchman may tire of correct and studied speech. I would advance this hypothesis as a tentative explanation for an expression that is now used throughout the country by the greatest and least of men, as a kind of catharsis or spiritual purgation that brings a conversation back to reality, as a prelude to its mounting again on the delicious wings of florid language. This expression—no doubt you have guessed the word already—we shall leave in French, not only because its meaning is quite clear, but because its counterpart in English, as in Spanish, is stronger and used for cursing. But in French it can mean "shucks," "darn it," or "pshaw." Accompanied by *alors,* it is even used to wish someone good luck. At one time, of course, the word did rank as a very harsh word even in French, but it rose to the heights of fame, thanks to its having been used by a general, and a Napoleonic general at that. When Cambronne was warned by his allies in the last phase of the Battle of Waterloo that further resistance was useless and that he ought to surrender, he grandly and vigorously declined with a single word: *Merde!* Immediately recalling that he was speaking for history, he hastened to add, "The Guard may die, but it does not surrender." Too late. What passed into history and into the language, the *mot de Cambronne,* was the other. And so the French managed to make a ribald expression famous.

And *argot?* A subterranean language, it exists at the margin of normal speech. Rather than besmirch the language of Racine with ugly and vulgar forms, the French have preferred to create another idiom, something like a sewer built along the edge of a great river. But thanks to their anxiety to publicize whatever seems characteristically French, they have given argot academic importance. The underworld speaks a special jargon in every great city, but they regard their lingo as something necessary,

PRIDE

not startling or particularly significant. In France, however, argot is mentioned with unmistakable respect; it is collected in dictionaries, and writers of the importance of Francis Carco study and publicize it.

> If it is not clear, it is not French.
>
> Rivarol, *Sur la Langue,* 1784.

The French treat their language as both wife and mistress, to avoid the temptations of any other. While speaking to a meeting of the International Council of the French Language at Versailles in 1968, Maurice Genevoix, Perpetual Secretary of the French Academy, pointed out that "God is better pleased by the oaths of a French soldier than by the prayers of an English parson." This was reported in *France-Soir,* and we believe it. Not the truth of the statement, but that the Secretary of the French Academy said it.

Voltaire wrote ironically: "They discussed the multiplication of tongues and reached the conclusion that, except for the misadventure of the Tower of Babel, the whole world would speak French." (*L'Ingenu,* Chapter 1.)

When a Frenchman in France finds it necessary to say something in English or some other language, he uses the fewest words possible to be understood. Since he feels it is monstrous that the other person doesn't speak French, he regards his communication as successful if it is comprehended, though not admired.

Like Southern belles visiting other parts of the United States, a Frenchman abroad makes no effort to lose his accent. If he happens to be with a sophisticated group of theater or movie people, he does the opposite, and tries to maintain it. In the United States I used to watch a personality named Geneviève regularly on the television show *Tonight.* With each year that passed her accent became more noticeable.

The waiters in New York's French restaurants act the same way. I feel sure that their accents are carefully scrutinized by the maître d's, and when they start to lose them as a result of speaking English to the natives, they are called on the carpet. Here, of course, we run up against American snobbishness, not just French pride. Rich Americans who go to La Caravelle like to be reminded by every word that they are in the center of continental cuisine and elegance.

When American soft drink companies tried to invade the French market after the war, they encountered stiff opposition, inspired in part by economic interests—the wine industry feared their potential competition—and in part by political considerations. The Communists and their fellow travelers, of course, could muster little enthusiasm for any American drink. But I heard other objections voiced with equal fervor by language purists. It seems that an American advertising agency had literally translated "Drink Coca-Cola" as *"Buvez Coca-Cola."* "Horrifying," exclaimed many writers and members of the Academy. "In French one must say *'Buvez* du *Coca-Cola'* or *'Buvez* le *Coca-Cola.'* "

The purists lost that battle and they are in the process of losing another. The pride of the French in their language has not been enough to stem the influx of English and particularly American words, even though the invasion is daily denounced, in vain, in the newspapers. The intruding expressions usually refer to commercial or social matters: the word "job" is used for a piece of work; the word "holding" is used by banks to describe holding companies; an ad for Pepsi-Cola displayed on a theater curtain described the beverage as *"le* drink *des raffinés";* elegant houses are said to show the high social "standing" of their occupants, just as elegant cars may do that are used for *"le* week end."

These English words are widely used. The French have satisfied their needs with their usual self-assurance, and they sprinkle the new words about in conversation without setting them off in quotes, as if they had been used by Corneille or Racine. Patriotically, they pronounce them

PRIDE

badly ("standing," for example, is accented on the last syllable), and one day they will no doubt discover that the words have been French all along. This wouldn't surprise me, because *Paris-Match,* taking note of the word rodeo used by American cowboys (which derives from the Spanish verb *rodear,* meaning "to round up" cattle for the purpose of driving them somewhere), ventured to speculate that surely the term evolved from the French expression *rendezvous.*

CULTURAL PRIDE

France has a great culture, but in addition the French know how to sell it better than anyone else. From the moment you cross their frontier or your plane lands at Orly, you become aware of a genuine atmosphere of culture: it's bound to impress anyone, oblivious though he may ordinarily be to spiritual matters. Tiny towns have several bookstores (Amélie-les-Bains has three in the space of a hundred yards); good popular libraries are found in every district of Paris. Aspects of culture that in other countries are the property of the few are within the reach of the majority in France. On the radio I used to hear daily afternoon cultural discussions at which books and authors were discussed—Chateaubriand, for example—that in other countries would be of interest only to scholars.

For the Frenchman, every spot is a good one for culture. France may be the only country in the world where skiing can be combined with short courses on the problems of our times, concerts of classical music, and showings of experimental movies. This is the program of the winter resorts at Courcheval, Flaine, Val-d'Isère, Arcs, and La Plagne, as reported with legitimate pride in *L'Express* of February 2, 1970.

The press caters to this interest or, even more, helps

create it with its news reports. Not only does every paper include special literary pages: literary matters often pop up in space that elsewhere is dedicated solely to political reporting. The deaths of Jean Paulhan and of François Mauriac were front page stories even in so low-brow a paper as *France-Soir*. The election of their successors to the French Academy was a matter of equal interest. Major literary prizes like the Goncourt, Renaudot, or Fémina are front page news, and the names of the leading candidates are bandied about to the point that they become the subject of betting. What a writer has to say—the *mot d'esprit* referred to earlier—is repeated over and over again, while the comment of one writer about another is retailed like a treasure. Madame Tessier, author of a famous column in *France-Soir* called "Neighborhood Gossip," very often mentions writers who would be familiar only to the elite in other countries because of the style or themes of their books.

The writers themselves have more than a little to do with the constant presence of their guild in the public eye, penning frequent open letters and treating each other with great respect even when their political positions are completely opposed. The Communist poet Aragon praises the Gaullist Mauriac, who praises the leftist atheist Sartre, who praises the style of the Catholic Paul Claudel to the skies. Faced with this behavior, the reader can hardly fail to conclude that he is dealing with the greatest writers in the world.

A similar kind of propaganda and emphasis is found in every cultural sphere. When a performance is about to begin in a Parisian theater, the foreigner may be surprised to see a dress uniform in the lobby. A guard in fine attire, complete with white gloves and a kepi hat, walks solemnly back and forth. This is symbolic of the state's attentiveness to literature. It doesn't matter if the play to be shown is little better than trivial vaudeville; the armed forces are there as the country's homage to culture.

As if a guard weren't enough to impress you, the ordi-

PRIDE

nary theater attendants behave with imposing ceremoniousness. Dressed in tuxedos, perched on a wooden stand, they look at you, when you arrive and hand them your ticket, with an air halfway between kindness and criticism, before they show you to your seat. "It seems as if they are going to inspect us," said the humorist Tono. At times a discrepancy may be observed between these rituals and the theater itself, which may be small, ugly, and inconvenient, with the seats too close together (see Avarice). Never mind, the point has been made: the French theater is something of importance.

France is good at selling her culture at home and very, very good at selling it abroad. French schools and institutes are located around the world for the purpose of spreading Gallic influence, and the budget for them, which is extremely high, has always been sacred, no matter who is in control of the government. The organization known as the Alliance Française maintains 1,200 language-teaching centers overseas and enrolls 500,000 students a year. The large expenses of this program are borne in part by the state and in part by citizens who buy "bonds" in response to such advertising slogans as the one I saw proclaiming, "For ten francs, ten Chilean children can attend a French lesson for one hour." The state also permits young men to escape military service by working instead as teachers of French in Africa or Asia.

At European universities, lecturers for the modern languages are often supplied by the countries where the languages are spoken; the men are sent out by the mother countries like so many extra consuls or commercial attachés. I have been Lecturer in Spanish at several institutions, and I asked university officials what happened when the embassies were requested to designate their lecturers for the following year. The French embassy was always the first to communicate the name of its lecturer and he was also the first to arrive, completely equipped with everything he might need for his mission: books to put on open reserve in the university library, a projector, slides, and maps. Besides, he was the best paid. (As for the other countries in my mini-survey, I found out that the English answered a little later and their lecturer arrived punctually but with a low salary. The Spanish government never replied, and the following year its lecturer would appear without warning, the payment of his salary having fallen six months in arrears.)

In Spain as in the United States, people are diffident about using the word "artist"; few dare to call themselves by that title. The word is in common use in France; in Montparnasse there is a Restaurant des Intellectuels et des Artistes. *"Donnez à l'artiste,"* says the fellow who has strummed his guitar in front of a sidewalk café, with complete seriousness.

France is the world's most powerful megaphone, rivaled, though unsurpassed, only by the United States. France creates reputations, spreads them, and even when people arrive on her shores already established, augments their fame. Joseph de Maistre remarked, "This is the nation where truths become universal," and his claim has a basis in fact.

Idea-truths and men-truths. If they are born in France they grow up under her care. If they are born abroad, they are taken in and nourished like members of the family. Think of the most important names in literature, art, or music today: Ionesco, a Rumanian; Beckett, Irish; Arrabal, Picasso, Dali, Spanish; Aznavour, Armenian; Yves Montand, Italian—all known throughout the world, but only after they had passed through Paris and been adopted by her.

Picasso's genius is completely Spanish, but the megaphone that broadcast his fame to every corner of the world was French, and the French have also paid him the highest honors. On his ninetieth birthday, an exhibition of his works was hung in the Louvre, which marked the first time the work of a living artist had been shown there. The exhibition was inaugurated by the President of France, who thanked the maestro from Málaga for having chosen his land as a place to live and work.

When it was proposed that a citizen of the United States, Julian Green, be elected to the French Academy, the dialectical skill of the Gauls blossomed in all its perfection. The opinion of a state agency consulted about the problem was that since Green had been born in Paris and could have chosen French nationality when he reached the age of eighteen, he could be considered French. The journalist Jaubert went even further in his reasoning: "While it is true that he did not petition for French nationality, it is also true that *he never refused it* . . . and besides, in the First World War he was a volunteer in the 32nd Artillery Regiment" (*Le Figaro,* May 7, 1971).

One might conclude that France as a nation takes advantage of foreigners and uses their talents to her own profit: that she is a usurper of nationalities and men. This is an easy charge to make, but unjust. First of all, the artists named and others like them came to Paris to find certain liberties that were sadly lacking in their own country: the political freedom to write and say what they wished, and the economic freedom to live as they liked. The first of these represents no special indulgence for artists; it corresponds to the broad-gauged way the French have had since the revolution of understanding all the problems of the world. Russian czarist or Italian anarchist, France lets in anyone who is not too hostile to the police.

In addition to the foreigners who are more or less integrated into French life, there are over 175,000 others in the country who are officially recognized as long-term visitors, and they are placed under the protection of an agency with the beautifully symbolic name, *Office Français de Protection de Réfugiés et Apatrides.* This tolerance is such a normal part of French civilization that its generosity is hidden under a bureaucratic coldness, which produces resentment in the refugees. In his novel *Marks of Identity,*

PRIDE

Juan Goytisolo portrays the attitudes of Spanish refugees in this regard. The thousands of refugees from the Civil War pass their days recalling the country which they were forced to leave and complaining about the land that took them in.

It is important to remember this in evaluating the propagandistic use France makes of foreign names. For every Picasso who gives the French something to boast about, they have thousands of refugees who bring them nothing but problems. To a certain extent the presence of good foreign artists and intellectuals compensates them for the money they pour into the bottomless well represented by the refugees.

The second interest—after freedom—of the artists who are "taken advantage of" in Paris is the full application of their ideas and energy to their art. This is what someone who triumphs in Paris achieves and what someone who works in Stockholm, Berlin, or Madrid fails to manage.

The spiritual vitality of the French can be seen with special clearness in their defeats. In 1945 they emerged from the war destroyed and divided; their political power was nil and their economy was in chaos. Sick in body and badly dressed, the only thing they had left was their brains. These they used to good purpose. Thanks to the works and wit of a group of thinkers led by Sartre, Europe became aware of a new doctrine that originally had been German. (This has often happened in French history. Ideas may arise somewhere else, but the French make themselves responsible for diffusing them.) The doctrine in question was Existentialism, and the early exportation of books explaining it marked the first victory of a people mired in the difficulties of the postwar period. Not until the works of Herbert Marcuse began to attract attention, twenty years later, would the world interest itself again so intensely in a few pages.

The French sell fashions as well as culture. While the doctrine of Existentialism was appealing to the natural pessimism felt by mankind after the war, a new style of dress that originated in the *caves de Saint-Germain* was sweeping victoriously around the world. Think a minute of what this triumph meant. The war had left Paris without coal; French women wore long pants in 1945 to fight off the cold, they let their hair fall straight and neglected because they didn't have money to go to the hairdresser's, and they spent hours and hours in the basement cafés of the Latin Quarter because these places were warmer than their houses.

The same patterns of behavior have developed at one time or another in every society of the world during moments of crisis. But the Parisians added one original touch: instead of being ashamed and hiding, they had their portraits painted while dressed this way, and they invented a style of living that by association came to be called existentialist. Within a few months the rich of North and South America, living in completely different social circumstances, dressed themselves in the same disheveled way. It takes powerful personality and great self-assurance to convert poverty—practically filth—into a world fashion.

(To show their power again, shortly thereafter they reversed their engines. At a time when clothing and money were scarce throughout the world, it occurred to Dior to launch the fashion of long dresses, in violation of every principle of logic and reason. Naturally, they succeeded. When has fashion needed the support of logic?)

In film they originated the New Wave. In the theater they created one new style with Ionesco and Beckett, another later with Arrabal. They even came up with the *nouveau roman,* Robbe-Grillet's new way of writing novels.

Cultural considerations are always present in the projects that the French undertake, even those that seem furthest from the purpose, like wars. When Napoleon was put in command of operations in Italy, the Directory gave him, along with a lot of other political and military instructions, an order to requisition the most beautiful works of art that he found in the Peninsula, so that the spirit of the French people might be enlarged to match their new borders.

As a matter of cold fact, then, in the realm of culture, French pride is on a solid foundation. They have placed pure thought on a lofty throne:

> "What a beautiful ball," said the count. "Nothing is missing."
> "Thought is missing," replied Altamira.
>
> *The Red and the Black,* Part II, Chapter 9.

Only in France have I ever seen an advertisement praise an automobile as being, not just comfortable, but "intelligent"—or heard parents bidding their child to be *sage* (wise) when they meant obedient and reasonable.

2 Avarice

NATIONAL MISERLINESS

"Stop, thief! Help, murder! I'm lost, dead, they've cut my throat, they've robbed me! Who could it have been? My money, my life, my dear friend, they've taken you from me.... I've lost my support, my consolation, my happiness. It's all over for me, without you I can't live. It's the end, I can't go on, I'm dying, I'm already dead, buried. Isn't there anyone who wants to revive me, to give it back? Dear money."

This is the end of the third act of Molière's *L'Avare*. It is dramatic because the miser uses the same expressions

A V A R I C E

in his complaints that someone else would use who had lost his wife or mother. He is the most famous of all French literary types and one of the best known in world literature.

World literature, of course, is replete with the caricatures of knaves and antisocial beings. But the curious and, to my way of thinking, symbolic thing about Molière's miser is that this pinchpenny fiend, this selfish monster who doesn't care a straw about his family or the happiness of his son or daughter, does not suffer the punishment at the end of the play that in other works marks the moral of the action. On the contrary, in exchange for a minimal concession—I say minimal because you can't compare the anxiety he feels for the young lady with that which he feels about his money—he recovers the latter and even avoids the expense of the wedding. Molière condemned Don Juan but saved the miser. Logically enough; the miser was just too French for Molière to deal harshly with him.

Had the miserliness of the French been spelled out only by their writers, we might have suspected an exaggeration, but the same information is supplied by their economists, a group famous for being coldly factual. When these scientists attempt to estimate the holdings of their countrymen, they almost always refer somewhere to the sums hidden in socks under the bed, a repository for funds still not completely replaced in modern times by banks or savings associations. The Frenchman enjoys saving as if it were an inexhaustible pleasure.

Armando Palacio Valdés, a Spaniard who demonstrated his great friendship for France during the First World War, did not hesitate to recall in one of his books some details about the Frenchman's love for his secret purse, which in various languages is called a "cat" or a "kitty":

> "France has a cat, we must take it from her," said Bismarck to his friends. Following his instructions, his disciples of today are trying to repeat the deed.
> There isn't a house in France, however poor, where

AVARICE

you can't find one of those felines, large or small, snoring in some neglected corner. I once met a municipal employee who supported a wife, a mother-in-law, and two children on a salary of 140 francs a month. Still and all, he confessed to me that he was able to hold out 15 francs a month for his cat. The day that a Frenchman couldn't give his pet at least a few scraps, he would die of jaundice.

The French habit of saving isn't sordid or repugnant; it is prudent, methodical, wise.... Saving is a passion in France, but it is a discreet and reserved passion, and people don't want to make a show of it, any more than old people in love want to display theirs. The French understand each other with a look when the subject comes up. A laborer or a clerk may head for the river with his fishing pole every Sunday after dinner. It appears to be a form of recreation, and this is the way he explains it. But the neighbors know what is at stake. "Monsieur X is going for his supper," they say to themselves. No one smiles; there is no joking. In France everything is worth a laugh except money.

In September of last year, M. Pierre, the barber, came home from the front on a four-day pass to the little town where I was spending the summer. He displayed the Croix de Guerre on his chest. What do you suppose that brave warrior did with his precious four days? He immediately opened the doors of his shop, which had been closed for more than a year, took off his coat, and started to shave his clients.

He told them how he had joined the attack, how he cut their throats, how they died. "In the name of God, watch out, you've nicked me," shouted his first client, and the barber suddenly became very scared. Why did that hero turn pale at the sight of a drop of blood, when he had seen so much flowing earlier and even had spilled a good deal himself? Ah! because that little drop sprang, not from some palpitating heart, but from his purse.

La guerra injusta, 1917.

AVARICE

Many years have gone by since this page was written, but the French haven't changed. At the first sign of any economic fluctuation, the rich hurry their money abroad and buy the strongest currency at the moment (most recently, the mark), but the immense majority of the French set about stuffing their cat with the only currency that they have trusted for generations: gold.

"The Stock Exchange is bearish, businessmen are short-tempered, and the majority in the Assembly is listless. The provinces hold their breath as they watch their wool socks. The gold Napoleon, that dollar of the countryside, will fly high this winter." (*L'Express,* December 9, 1968.)

Numerous proverbs put one on guard against the terrible vice called generosity. Here is M. de Rênal, a character in *The Red and the Black,* explaining his ideas about trees: "I like shade.... I have *my* trees trimmed so that they give shade. What else is a tree good for? They don't make any money."

Stendhal makes use of the occasion to attack the stinginess of all of provincial France, as reflected in his imaginary town of Verrières:

> Here we have the phrase that decides everything in Verrières: *to make money.* It is the single constant thought of three-quarters of the inhabitants.
>
> Making money is the criterion that decides everything in this little town that seems so beautiful to you. The stranger who first arrives here, enchanted by the beauty of the cool, deep valleys surrounding the town, may imagine that the inhabitants are very sensible to beauty, since they speak so often of the beauty of the land. One can't deny that they make a fuss about it, but the reason is that this attracts strangers whose money enriches the hotel keepers and indirectly, by way of licenses and taxes, makes money for the town.
>
> *The Red and the Black,* Book I, Chapter 2.

"What is called generosity is often nothing better than the vanity of giving." This is one of La Rochefoucauld's

AVARICE

"reflections" (1665). To avoid this vanity, it's best not to give too much and to save as much as possible.

One thing you can say for French avarice, the French are completely free of hypocrisy about it. Their intention to pile up a fortune, giving as little as possible and taking in all they can, is crystal clear to the tourist the minute he sets foot in the country.

If you ask for a cup of coffee, they give you a few minuscule lumps of sugar. It's true, they don't insist that you just use one, but if you don't mind partly sweetened coffee, why should you add more? A sign on the wall of a bar warns that after midnight, everything costs 20 per cent more. Ask for imported whisky or gin in Paris. In the bottom of the glass you will note a small quantity. They haven't in fact given you a dirty glass with the liquor the previous client neglected to finish; it's just the normal serving of whisky in the country. I figured out the cost of a bottle and it came to the same price as in Spain; remembering that the French, with their stronger economy, have a much easier time raising this amount of money, the conclusion is obvious. Either the Spaniards are the most generous people in the world or the French are the tightest. A comparison with Germany or Italy will tell us which half of the proposition explains the situation in France. "What makes us happy is not being rich, but getting rich" (Stendhal, *Vie de Rossini,* 1824).

If jokes are social documents, the cartoon I saw in *Paris-Match* was, without its author meaning it to be, a denunciation. A young lady is eating in a restaurant. She drops her fork, and three gentlemen come rushing over from neighboring tables to pick it up, apparently to return it to her. The question is this: in what sort of European restaurant does a person go on eating with a fork that has fallen on the floor?

AVARICE

When they started to give obligatory flu shots in various corporations many people complained. As one typist put it, "Why should I give the boss back a whole week of sick leave?" (*L'Express,* November 2, 1970.)

French stinginess sometimes shows up in cramped facilities. Even in fairly good restaurants the tables and chairs are tiny so that more people can be fitted in, forcing one almost to eat sideways to avoid bumping other customers. Even in luxurious establishments like the Crazy Horse the tourists are packed in almost on top of one another. When you eat alone, you are taken to a table next to the door where it would be absolutely impossible to seat another client. Couples go to tables made for two, trios to tables that seat three and no more. The sight of a table that seats four at which only three were eating would give the owner apoplexy.

When you order a dinner in Paris you may feel like turning down half the things that come with it. I've done so many times. No matter: the bill arrives with no discount. *"Le repas à prix fixe c'est ça,"* and that's that. At other times I've turned down the French fries that come with the meat and asked for a vegetable instead; even though I didn't want several other items included with the dinner, I wound up having to pay a franc extra because vegetables are more expensive than potatoes. What about the dishes I didn't eat? Ah, Monsieur, that's your business.

Miserliness can lead to rudeness. Impresarios, for instance, don't pay their ushers very well, and they therefore have to make up the deficiency by demanding, not asking, tips from the customers. *"Le service, Monsieur!"* is a national cry. On my first visit to Paris and, naturally, at the Folies Bergère, I was astonished to hear, when I tried to enter the men's room, an attendant demanding very dryly, *"Le service, Monsieur!"* (She didn't wait until you were leaving: that way you might get away without paying. Her power was in not letting people in, and she knew it.)

In some places I've read a notice that says "Tipping is at the discretion of the clientele." But unless your tip

AVARICE

amounts to a franc or more, you won't be thanked, even if the centimes you left amount to 20 per cent of the bill.

This dryness and hardness is explained, I might add, by the people's pride. A person who has to ask for something is always humiliated, no matter how much of a national institution the tip may be, and the way the French hide their humiliation is to demand as a right what is really a favor.

Tipping extends to unlikely situations. If you buy a program in the theater you have to tip for *service* besides, and the same is true of the checkroom after you've paid the stated fee to reclaim your coat. Along this road there is no natural stopping place: there's no reason at all why the clerk who sells you a shirt shouldn't demand a tip as well.

In a restaurant in the Place du Tertre, two young ladies tired of calling the *patronne* to take their money. Finally, they left their money on the table and started for the door. *"Un moment!"* shouted the owner, *"Je vais vérifier!"* And she counted it, loudly pronouncing the numbers, while the girls waited at the door, visibly upset.

In another restaurant in Montparnasse I sent back a steak because it was bad. When the check arrived they charged me for it and also the steak that had replaced it. Was it possible? *"Ah, oui,* if all our customers acted the way you did, how could we stay in business?"

French avarice is so widespread that everyone understands it and no one lets himself get sentimental about acts of generosity, in which they always suspect a trick. "Sometimes an unselfish, disinterested act is only an investment at higher interest than usual," said d'Houdenot in 1853.

Any sort of attack on a Frenchman's savings produces an incredible uproar. In September 1968 there was talk of raising inheritance taxes, and many commentators warned the government that this would be political suicide. "Tax things sold on the street," the author of one article advised; "raise the prices of whatever the French still haven't bought, but be very careful about taking away any of the money that they already have at home. One's

51

AVARICE

inheritance is sacred because it is something on which one already counts." Perhaps his cry of alarm was heard, because the law as signed was much less harsh than had been proposed.

Once while I waited my turn in a wine store I overheard a conversation between the proprietor and the owner of another establishment. Judging by the gravity of their tone, I gathered that they were speaking about a major swindle. They shook their heads vigorously from side to side. *"Ah, non!"* they said, *"ah, non, ça alors!"* Where will it end? Horrible, horrible, absolutely intolerable. It turned out that they were talking about a check that some soulless scoundrel—that was the kindest name they gave him—had tendered in the barbershop on the corner and which bounced because of insufficient funds. It was for twenty francs, about four dollars, but to judge by how scandalized the shopkeepers were, you would have thought it was England's great train robbery. What an outrage! They refused even to consider the possibility that some day one of their own checks might bounce through a similar oversight. They demanded the sternest punishment for the miserable wretch capable of taking advantage of someone in this way. I reflected that in other countries allowance is made for small losses of this sort, but those good Frenchmen were not disposed to permit the slightest shortfall in their income.

And at the theater? The seats are minuscule, the leg room between rows is practically nonexistent and a torture for anyone but a midget, and now they have invented *transportines,* seats that fold down into the aisles at the end of each row. In some theaters—the Michèle, for example—other seats fold down from the walls. As a result, when the show begins, the aisles are completely filled, and the danger in case of fire is apparent. Does the impresario have any thoughts about this? "What does this possible risk of fire count for compared to the risk of a heart attack I run when I spot an empty space in a sold-out theater?"

AVARICE

The materialism of the French has repercussions in politics. During the upheaval of May 1968 many residents along the Boulevard Saint-Germain started out by helping the students, even throwing water on the tear gas canisters launched by the police to lessen their effect. Three days later, some of these good bourgeois citizens who had been so amused by the revolution that their children were trying to start, began firing BB guns from their balconies at the students on the barricades. What had transpired? The rebels had burned a few cars belonging to their erstwhile supporters and this seemed completely stupid and unjust to the average Frenchman. As soon as they had a chance, they rushed out to vote for de Gaulle, so that he could defend them a few years longer against these ferocious enemies of private property. Later they would continue ensuring their property by voting for Pompidou.

The Frenchman complains constantly about conditions, but he hasn't any interest in seeing the conditions change if this will cost him money. In a poll about public transportation taken by *L'Express* in February 1970, 50 per cent of the respondents were sure that conditions had gotten worse, and 11 per cent defined the extent of the deterioration as "scandalous." When they were asked whether they were ready to pay a little more so that these deficiencies might be corrected, 47 per cent said no and 25 per cent said they were uncertain. Asked if they would pay more taxes so that public transportation might be free, 49 per cent said emphatically that they would not and 29 per cent said they were uncertain.

Not even love can escape from this miserliness. "Love is worth a lot, but money buys everything," goes a proverb traced back to 1558. "A suitor without a fortune may be worthy of love but he can't be happy," added Florian.

In the nineteenth century a song of Pierre Dupont's

AVARICE

became famous—no one was ever more French than he—
that went as follows:

> J'aime Jeanne ma femme
> eh bien j'aimerais mieux
> voir mourir ma Jeanne
> que voir mourir mes boeufs!

> (I love Jeanne my wife, but then I'd rather see
> Jeanne lose her life, than see my oxen die.)

Anyone might have thought of this song; songs like it probably have appeared in several other countries around the world. The matter becomes serious only when such a song proves to be popular.

> Generosity consists less in giving a lot than in giving
> at the right moment.
>
> La Bruyère, *Les Caractères,* 1688.

It's beautiful to arrive at the movies when the lights are on and the theater is half empty. Obviously, the usher then has no role to play, as my friend pointed out (see Pride), but the French girls who have the job are not intimidated. Usually when they see that you are vacillating between sitting in the rear with fewer people or up front to get a better view of the screen, they make a generous gesture: "I'll let you choose . . ." and then they put out their hand for a tip, which they deposit in a curious purse attached to their wrist, one that jangles in time with their steps.

In an interview, the ushers had their chance to complain about everyone else. "I answered an ad for ushers, they gave me a uniform to try on, and luckily enough it fit. They accepted me."

"What do you mean, 'luckily'?"

"Yes, because if it hadn't been my size, they wouldn't have taken me, because then the management would have had an extra expense." (*Parispoche,* January 21, 1970.)

The quest for the customer's money never stops and anyone who thinks that once he's bought his ticket he's safe is completely mistaken. Besides having to tip the usher, the checkroom girl, the program vendor, and the washroom attendant, the visitor finds himself besieged by vendors who harass the people who choose not to go out to the lobby during intermission. In the Folies Bergère and places like it, the audience is invited to spend the intermission viewing a belly dance in the basement; one pays extra for this, of course, as also for another program, another tip, and a little rubber doll that dances the rumba when you press her hips.

The miser is suspicious by nature because he sees every act as an attempt to take something from him. The best French pedagogues have warned their readers of the risks they run when they perform any generous act. In the sixteenth century, in *Notables enseignements: Adages et proverbes,* 1568, Gabriel Meurier advised, "Cut down a hanging man, he'll hang you" *(Dépends un pendard, il te pendra).* A couple of centuries later, La Fontaine pointed out in one of his fables that "Mistrust is the mother of security" *(La Méfiance est mère de la sûreté).* If so, why should we trust anyone? Collect in advance when you can.

At a meal in Spain, the guests usually linger quite a while after finishing; they don't want to seem rude by appearing to have come to the house just to eat. In France, the contrary is true: good manners dictate that you leave the minute lunch is finished. A guest who attempts to prolong the conversation after dessert is likely to notice a certain coldness in his hosts, and not because he has said something indiscreet. The reason is simply that, besides the meal, he is costing his hosts their time.

Speaking of food, sharing it is not one of the Frenchman's weaknesses when he is in a train or some other public place. I can give a dramatic instance to back this up, one reported to me by some people who could hardly believe it, though they had seen it with their own eyes. During the Second World War, Spaniards still detained in the jails of Paris as a result of their own Civil War were

AVARICE

astonished to see their French cellmates eating food sent by their relatives—something that never befell the Spaniards, for obvious reasons—without offering them a bite. When they finished, they expounded to the Spaniards about the excellent qualities of the food!

Within the general context of his usual avarice, the Frenchman is able to discriminate about tips. If the person tipping him is his countryman, he can accept a smaller amount. When the giver is a foreigner, a man he has already honored more than enough by serving him delicacies he neither deserves nor appreciates, it is inadmissible that the tip should not be very large.

A typical incident proving this difference happened to Valentin Parera, the widower of the famous American singer Grace Moore and a man perfectly accustomed to life in Paris. In a restaurant he saw a couple give the *sommelier* 100 francs—old francs, of course. The sommelier bowed his thanks. When Valentin's turn came to pay, he gave the same amount, which was accepted with an icy *merci*. The Spaniard at once asked him to return the tip, and then explained to the astonished man why he did so.

"Those people gave you the same amount as I did and you fawned all over them. Why are you so disrespectful to me? Because I'm not French? I've suffered enough already, for heaven's sake."

And he marched out with a dignified look.

A French saying goes, *"Mon verre est petit, mais je bois dans mon verre"* (My glass is little but I'll drink from it). His glass is little, true enough—all you have to do is go up to a bar to see that—but the egoism of the proverb is interesting. A Frenchman's glass is his property and no one has any reason to touch it. When the French discovered the house trailer or *caravane* they were very happy. It allowed them to leave home without completely abandoning their house, and they saved a sum of money important to the hotels of the country by carrying their own glass. At present there are 250,000 caravanes in France, or one for ev-

AVARICE

ery 205 Frenchmen, a very high proportion. As everyone knows, French highways are narrow, but this doesn't matter. At the wheel of the towing vehicle, a Frenchman is completely happy, and if no one can pass him because the mass of his moving house blocks off all vision of the road ahead, that's just too bad.

Every country in the world has recently made an effort to improve its hotel facilities in order to attract tourists who bring in foreign exchange and give jobs to many people. In France, pride, discussed earlier, has combined with avarice to keep the French from doing more than necessary. Hotels along the highways are nearly nonexistent, and the French absolutely refuse to modernize the few there are so long as they don't actually fall to pieces. If a foreigner happens to be fooled by the agreeable aspect of some of these buildings—red-tile roofs, white walls, flowers on lattices—and stops his car at one of them, he runs head on into their faults. The conversation with the owner is likely to develop more or less as follows:

"Do you have an empty room, by any chance?"

"Well, yes, I have one left. For how many days?"

"Just tonight. Does it have a bath?"

Hardly has this question escaped before the traveler regrets it. The owner is shaking her head and turning red in the face. Not that she's blushing because the room doesn't have a bath. She is enraged because the question seems absolutely out of place, and quite offensive. *"Ah, non, Monsieur, pas de salle de bain.* That's all we'd need, to have a bathroom in every room. Good Lord, good Lord. Besides, didn't you say that you were going to stay for just one night? Then why do you need a bath?"

The situation is clear enough. Her avarice did not permit her to install a bathroom, but her pride resented the fact that a miserable foreigner dared to suppose that having such a service was only normal. No, sir; if the French don't have baths in their motels, then it's normal, do you understand? normal, not to have them. The Americans who demand them are simply barbarians. And furthermore, there is no heat. *"Je ne chauffe pas!"*

The Frenchman's limited capacity for spending shows up in the statistics compiled for the tourist industry in Spain. French tourists constitute 40 per cent of the total visiting their neighboring country, but they account for only 20 per cent of the money spent there. After interviewing many Frenchmen who had visited Spain—I passed myself off as an American when I talked to them—my personal opinion is that their reasons for going there on their vacations were (1) low cost (2) the sun and (3) the landscape, bullfights, and flamenco dances. But between the first and second reasons there was a tremendous gap.

According to Spanish waiters, French travelers are the only ones who ask for a single paella dish for two or even four people.

A French travel agent reports, "My French clients have a fixed idea: pay less than anyone else while visiting a place farther away."

> Virtue without money is a useless ornament.
>
> Boileau, *Epître,* 1669.

The Frenchman stops being a miser only when he can enrich himself with relative ease. The lure of betting attracts him because the possibility of winning a lot with a little outweighs his fear of losing a small sum, and so the French language has given the world many gambling terms. The *roulette* wheel is used everywhere, and the *croupier* says *"Faites vos jeux, Messieurs."* The lottery is very popular. Newspapers print yesterday's winning *tiercé* (a bet that specifies the first three horses in a race) on page one, and all the race results are reported in infinitely greater detail than discussions in the Chamber of Deputies.

To lose something he has counted on is a grave matter for a Frenchman. The most violent demonstrations in France in the months following the student uprising of May 1968 were between farmers and small businessmen and the police. Thirty injuries were recorded in Paris in October 1969. The farmers were outraged about the low prices for their vegetables in the marketplace and about how little the government was doing to protect them in their hour of need. The small businessmen felt that they were being choked out by the large supermarkets and pushed under by the social security contributions that the government had imposed on all businesses, even the family-run store, under pressure from the Left. When Pompidou, after devaluing the franc, sent inspectors to make sure that prices did not go up, this category of Frenchmen took it as a personal insult. (In 1958, the small businessmen had managed to defeat legislation that would have required a cash register in every business establishment. What lack of confidence did that measure show? And besides, how was the businessman to cheat the tax collector with such a machine around?)

Poujade was the symbol of this attitude and he had considerable influence in his time. *Poujadisme,* according to Jean Riverain, is a "political attitude of small businessmen and property owners who think only of their own immediate interests." The movement took its name from Pierre Poujade, founder of the Union for the Defense of the Businessmen and Artisans of France. "*Poujadisme* is a constant in the French temperament," Riverain concluded (*Les Nouvelles Littéraires,* December 4, 1969).

Early in November 1970 *Le Figaro* took a poll to determine which liberties were valued most highly by the French. In ascending order, the respondents mentioned an independent judiciary (this got the least votes), the right to have political parties, the right to strike, freedom of the press. . . .

But the right that seemed much the most important to the Frenchmen interviewed was the right to receive a social security pension.

AVARICE

Another inquest, this one reported by *Paris-Match* (November 17, 1969), dealt with the Europe of the future. To the question, "If Europe is united politically, would you be disposed to accept the principle of collective diplomacy and defense for all countries of the Common Market?" some 66 per cent enthusiastically said yes, and this voluntary limitation of French rights was repeated in answer to an even bolder question. "If a president of Europe were to be elected, would you vote for a foreign candidate whose political program corresponded to your own ideas better than the program of a French candidate?" Again, 66 per cent indicated that they were more European than chauvinistic.

But further along another question appeared: "If it were necessary in order to construct a united Europe, would you accept a small lessening of your buying power for a few years?" *Non,* 48 per cent of the Frenchmen interviewed stated emphatically, while another 17 per cent declined to answer at all.

Which tends to show that the Frenchman finds it easier to sacrifice national pride than his personal avarice.

Frenchmen, de Gaulle pointed out in his comments about Erlanger's book *Richelieu,* love magnificence and even worship it, but only in retrospect. In their own time, they are horrified by its cost and are unwilling to sacrifice their comfort for undertakings that hold promise of bringing incalculable benefits to their children.

The French take such pleasure in mentioning large sums that they resisted changing their methods of accounting when the currency was reformed and one new franc replaced one hundred old ones. For years after the changeover, the papers continued to announce prizes, public expenditures, an inheritance, or the income of a movie star according to the old formula. They always chose to say 100 million instead of 100 thousand, though they had to add A.F. (for *anciens francs*).

One incident in the history of France seems particularly reasonable and logical to everyone. It happened during

AVARICE

the Wars of Religion. The people were killing and being killed over different ways to pray to Jesus Christ and the deaths were generally pretty disagreeable: impalement, burning at the stake, drawing and quartering. In this atmosphere of fanaticism and fighting to the death, the Parisians, partisans of the Catholic League of the Guises, were supported within their city by Spanish troops, stationed there as allies in the struggle against the Huguenot Henry of Navarre. They faced a difficult choice. Patriotism urged them to be governed by a French prince and not by the Spaniard Philip II, but their religion was against it. They brought their dilemma to Henry, who arranged everything with a smile, announcing his conversion. His comment has passed into history: "Paris is worth a Mass."

Was it worth it? No, if you believe more in the recompenses of the afterlife than in material gains. But for a Frenchman with a chance to obtain Paris and with it, the crown, heavenly bliss wasn't in the running. No French historian has ever criticized him for his decision, not even Protestant ones, because placed in the same situation they would probably have done the same thing. Remember the contradictory, naturally less practical phrase of Philip II when he was faced with the Calvinist uprising in Flanders: "I would rather lose my kingdoms than rule over heretics." He lost them, of course.

> A rich peasant is better than a poor gentleman.
>
> Marthurin Regnier, *Satires,* 1608.

In the little town of Saint-Pierre-les-Nemours a tragedy occurred: a married couple named Lelièvre killed all their children. Newsmen from all over Europe converged on the site. To one of them the butcher commented, "The Lelièvres? I only wish all my customers were like them. Not a penny in debt."

France would now have a hundred million inhabitants if the growth rate of the nineteenth century had continued. But when the right of primogeniture was abol-

AVARICE

ished, the rich landowning class feared that their lands would be dispersed and began to practice the system of having a single son, just like the bourgeoisie.

In a recent book entitled *The Snakes of Paris,* a Frenchman studied the characteristic vice of his compatriots with a wealth of anecdotes. The one about a famous tenor who took his friends out to dinner will suffice. After the last course, the maître d' inquired, "Would the gentlemen like cheese?" "They like it," intervened the singer, "but they've already had it in the minestrone soup."

One of the most French of French writers is Guy de Maupassant, an artist admired equally by literary critics and by the public, who devoured his books as they appeared, especially the collections of short stories, which continually reflect anxiety about money. "At Sea" relates the adventure of a shipowner who lets a cable destroy his brother's arm rather than cut it, since it cost 1,500 francs. In "The Tramp," a rich man tells a beggar, "I gave you a piece of bread three days ago. I'm not going to feed you all year long!" Unfortunately, the author reminds us, the beggar had to eat all year long. So he kills a chicken, is given a thrashing, and goes to jail. Another example of harshness appears in "Pierrot." The story's title is the name of a dog, purchased as protection against robbers by a rich old lady who lives with her maid. The dog is too friendly to strangers, and besides, the authorities try to collect a fee for a license, so the old woman throws the dog in a deep hole, where it howls for days. When her neighbors try to charge her four francs to get the dog out, she decides at least to help him a little by throwing down food, but later another larger dog is thrown in and it eats the first dog's food. "I'm not going to feed all the dogs they throw in there," says the woman, and she departs with her maid, leaving her dog.

In "In the Country," a poor family gives one of its two children to a rich couple without heirs. When, years later, the adopted boy returns in his coach to see his real parents, the other boy, kept by his loving mother and sharing the hardships of his parents' life, cries at them indignantly, "That could have been me!"

Harshness, egotism, and hard-heartedness are reflected in other de Maupassant stories. In "The Little Barrel," a worker makes an arrangement with the owner of a house to live in it until he dies. The owner then proceeds to stimulate his alcoholism, giving him more and more casks of wine until he dies. In "Rempailleuse," a chair-caner loves a boy all her life and leaves him all her money when she dies. The haughty boy and his wife are annoyed about the ambitious and impertinent chair-caner until they hear of her bequest. "Since it was her last wish it would be difficult to refuse it," the couple concludes. "Perhaps we can buy something for the children."

Carrying French avarice to the level of comedy, de Maupassant tells us the story of "Toine," the old invalid whose wife, tired of serving him and getting nothing in return, obliges him to use his forced immobility in bed for something useful: to hatch chicken eggs. (These stories are all among the thirty-six included in the volume *Contes choisis: Édition pour la jeunesse.*)

Yes, the ancient, eternal capital sin of the French is avarice. French writers have realized it all along. Montherlant, in his play *La Ville dont le prince était un enfant,* gives a tremendous line to the headmaster of a school: "Generosity. God knows our country needs it."

Another hero of French literature, stingier and even more repugnant than Molière's, appears in Balzac's *Eugénie Grandet* (1833). When people reminded Balzac that Eugénie's father had an antecedent in the seventeenth century, he commented, "Molière portrayed a miser. I portrayed miserliness." And he was right. Here is how Eugénie's father spent his last days.

> Eugénie put his gold louis on the table, and he spent hours on end with his eyes fixed on the coins, like a child who stupidly goes on contemplating the same object the moment he begins to see.

AVARICE

"This revives me," he said from time to time, letting a blissful expression pass over his face.

When the parish priest came to administer the last rites, his eyes, seemingly dead for hours, were reanimated at the sight of the cross, the candelabras, and the silver cup of sacred water. When the priest offered him the enameled cross he made a terrible effort to grasp it.

"Bet on faith and you will come out well. If God exists you will have won your way into Paradise. If he doesn't, you won't have lost a thing." So says Pascal.

Voltaire made a similar religious calculation when he built a church chapel on his Ferney estate with the inscription "Voltaire built it for God." Reminded that it was more usual to dedicate a church to a saint, not God, the philosopher answered, "It's always better to address yourself to the master than to his servants."

3 Lust

NATIONAL REPUTATION

When we think of nations we associate human characteristics with them, and clichés—many times just ones—are formed. And so every time we hear a country mentioned, an association of ideas occurs. Some countries do all they can to live up to their reputations.

This is the case with France. The country is commonly regarded as a perfect synonym for lovemaking, particularly the lovemaking that leads speedily to sensualism (the "French kiss"), vice ("French style" suggests various perversions), and punishment for carnal sins (syphilis was called the "French disease" in centuries past). To say "French" is to call up visions of naked ladies and cuckolded husbands. Someone who says "I've got a French girl friend" can count on an exchange of leering winks by everyone around him. "So she's French, hah?" A few years back *Esquire* published a cartoon showing a wealthy man returning from work to his elegant home. His wife is at the door to meet him, and she says, "The new maid is here, French, just as you wanted." The man's face glows with lascivious anticipation. In the doorway behind the wife, however, we see the maid: ugly, short, bowlegged, squinting cross-eyed through thick glasses—the opposite, in sum, of what a man anywhere in the world would imagine when he hears a French girl mentioned.

France cultivates her reputation so diligently that one can't be sure whether she acts this way because she believes it's true or because she feels she must pay tribute to it. Notice, to begin with, that in the concert of nations all priding themselves on their virility, France boasts of her femininity. The country's coat of arms shows a rooster crowing, and we know that the rooster is a symbol of sexual domination, but when French cartoonists are looking for a way to represent their country in a drawing they always choose sweet young Marianne, the girl with the regional dress and Phrygian cap. She is usually shown as disconcerted by the violent behavior of John Bull, Uncle Sam, Hans the German, or fur-capped Ivan.

The latest proof of the feminization of the French symbol is the bust of Marianne carved in the unmistakable shape of Brigitte Bardot. The first official to choose this version for his office in city hall was the mayor of Thiron-Gardais, a small town (six hundred inhabitants) in Normandy, but many others have since followed his example, sharing the convictions of the statue's creator, the sculptor Aslan. "I noticed," said Aslan, "that all these Mariannes in government offices had Greek profiles, a ridiculous feature in a statue meant to represent the French Republic. B.B., who really is a symbol of France, seems much more appropriate." (*Herald Tribune,* Paris, March 8, 1971.)

LUST

The graphic panorama presented by the cartoonists and image makers of France makes it easy for her citizens to deduce that unhappy Marianne is once again the victim of the concupiscence of her neighbors, and so international problems are transformed into sexual ones. Doubtless the interpretation is warranted in some cases. Germany invades France every X years with the blind impetuosity of a lover who decides on rape after his attempts to achieve an honorable marriage have been scorned. The mechanically rhythmic footsteps of the Wehrmacht are those of a rapist who has just broken down the closely guarded doors of the manor and now strides toward the bedroom. When Hitler arrived in Paris a few days after its occupation, he gazed on the Place de la Concorde for a long time from his balcony in the Hotel Crillon. *"Das ist eine Sonate,"* he murmured. Yes, it is a sonata, but the observation was the most precious that a German music devotee could say to his beloved. And this same love, tinged with respect, that the barbarian felt for the country he had raped caused Hitler to attempt a marriage of convenience with France, thus blocking the Irredentist schemes of the Duce and failing to meet Franco's demands for Morocco as a condition for entering the war. As happens in some instances of human violation, the German leader wanted afterward to please and pamper the victim of his attack. And France, again as happens in daily life, did everything she could to take vengeance on her violator, alternatively using a shield (Pétain) and a sword (de Gaulle).

International politics, ordinarily so masculine an activity, seem in this case tinged with a disconcerting sensualism. But sensualism also invades French society in general. Consider the French verb *aimer,* which means both "to love" and "to like" or "to be fond of." English distinguishes the two concepts with separate words, and so do Spanish *(querer, gustar),* German *(lieben, gefallen),* and Italian *(amare, piacere),* but French uses one verb for both meanings indiscriminately. This first struck me when I heard a bearded scholar, a specialist in the French Revolution, assure me, *"J'aime Robespierre."* When the director of the Odeón theater, Jean-Louis Barrault, was expelled from his post by André Malraux for his behavior during the events of May, Maurice Escande, administrator of the Comédie Française, resolved his conflict of duties in these terms: *"J'aime beaucoup Barrault; j'aime aussi, énormément, le ministre."*

Everything feminine in France is prized as a delicious treasure. The national hero of the country is a heroine; the French are proud to match Jeanne d'Arc, the Maid of Orleans, against the Saint Georges and Jameses of other countries. In the grammar of their language, even the army is a feminine word. It's the only country I know where orators mention women twice at the start of every speech: *"Mesdames, Mesdemoiselles, Messieurs. . . ."* This interest lies at the root of their ability to launch styles in jewels, perfumes, and clothing for the entire world. Typically, fashion is protected by law in France, and copying an article of clothing is punished about as severely as cracking a safe. Such seriousness in frivolous matters is characteristic of the French.

In 1962 I crossed the Atlantic on the liner *France*. The voyage was her inaugural run between Cherbourg and New York. The French hadn't made the *France* the largest ship in the world (it fell below the Queens in tonnage), but to satisfy their pride they had achieved another kind of primacy for her by making her the longest ship, by a few yards. Advertisements about the ship lyrically described its details.

The cabins were naturally a prodigy of decoration. Telephone communications, on the other hand, left much to be desired, and I couldn't find a photograph of the ship to illustrate the article I was writing about her. I noted other deficiencies, many traceable to the fact that this was the first voyage, but in my cabin I discovered a bottle of cologne for the men, a bottle of perfume for the women, and this sign, as French as it could be: "Ladies are advised that the light in this cabin is exactly the same as in the salons and the dining room." The shipbuilders had overlooked nothing in their desire to accommodate the requirements of makeup, women, and love.

It seems likely, of course, that a person's surroundings affect his relations with the opposite sex. At least this is the theory advanced by a new school of interior decoration: "Obstinately austere, interior decoration today opposes its barriers of glass, steel, and virginal white to the impulses of the heart. Modern rooms are too rigorous, too disciplined, too clean—how can you make love in them?"

A grave problem, and one dealt with even more forthrightly by the decorator Isabelle Hebey: "The city man is directly threatened by impotence or difficulty in making love. To meet this challenge, he needs to find in the framework of his daily life everything that can incite him to abandon himself." Which means touches of fur on the ironwork, comfortable furniture, lights that seem to travel over the clouds, and so forth. To find out whether modern man can achieve his objective in this way, read the rest of the article in *L'Express* of January 12, 1970.

Love, or at least amorous sentiment, continually surfaces in a Frenchman's gestures. No other people touch so often. Lovers kiss each other on the mouth whenever they feel like it in any street in Paris, sometimes interrupting the flow of pedestrians. Foreigners, particularly Spaniards or Italians, stop and watch in amazement, but this reaction is so unusual that the French stop to look at *them*. Women kiss each other on the cheek two and even three times: one cheek, the other, and back to the first. Fathers and mothers kiss their children whenever they spot them during the day, although they may have said good-bye only an hour before, and when a medal is awarded to some worthy gentleman, a kiss on both cheeks with much brushing of mustaches against the skin is an obligatory ritual.

When the occasion isn't right for kissing they shake hands. Pierre Daninos pointed out this obsession, which leads them to stop right in the middle of the street, where they risk being run over by traffic, simply to press each other's hands. I used to eat in Paris at a neighborhood restaurant near the Place des Vosges where a certain group of workers met every day for lunch. Many of them, I could tell from their conversation, had been working all morning in the same factory bay. It didn't matter. Each new arrival circled the table, leaning over it when necessary, to grasp the hands stretched out toward him. *Salut, salut,* again and again. In the Racing Club of Paris, where I took fencing, the class was interrupted so that the teacher could shake hands with whoever came up to say hello. A simple nod of the head from afar would have been interpreted as a tremendous discourtesy.

And when no humans are around they establish contact with dogs. The *Reader's Digest* reports that 29 per cent of French homes have dogs, 25 per cent have cats. A lady kissing Chouchou and showering words of affection on him is a common sight in any French café. And to say good-bye to them forever, they use much more affectionate phrases than you find in cemeteries for people, as the cemetery for dogs in Asnières, on the outskirts of Paris, clearly shows. Here are some of the inscriptions:

> Here lies Didi and so I am alone,
> believing in nothing.

This union of religious faith with love for a dog transcends the limits of death. There will be a place, as Bécquer's verse describes it, "where the closing sepulchre opens an eternity, and we shall have to discuss everything that we kept silent before." Let's see:

> Beloved Lulu:
> Since you left me forever
> Our house is empty, life is sad
> And I bear my sorrow.
> How dearly would I love to see you.
> If this wish were granted,
> Death would seem sweet to me:
> Only death can erase your beloved memory.

LUST

This one was signed properly "G.B." Other inscriptions have a lightly romantic touch:

> Hera, you loved the sea,
> May the Seine cradle your final sleep.

Sometimes a photo shows the owner next to his dog. Other photos show a married couple united in sorrow.

> You gave us thirteen years of happiness.
> You were gay, sweet, and tender.

One couple promised something that often isn't carried out when the fallen party is a human being:

> When we stop coming to see you
> It will mean that we are dead.
> Never will we replace you.

Love in France is so closely associated with the sexual act that the word is always ambiguous. *Faire l'amour* is an act that normally takes place in the privacy of a bedroom, although its translations in English ("to make love," "to make love to someone") can signify an attempt to achieve a more or less platonic relationship.

Amour is so important in France, it affects the standing of great personages with the public. "The mistresses of Louis XIV," remarked a critic reviewing a book about them, "are part of our national glory. They should find their place in our schoolbooks." ("La littérature érotique d'aujourd'hui," *Magazine Littéraire,* December 1967.) The basic research to support such a development is now going forward: first-rate scholars are busily scrutinizing the beds of yesteryear, trying to discover the least details about the liaisons of the past, and publishing interesting books: *The Great Lovers of History, Histories of Love in France* ("love" always in the sense previously discussed), *Bedroom Secrets from Other Times,* etc.

Occasionally the sexual conduct of the chief of state has earned the attention of his subjects. Francis I and Henry IV, the *vert galant,* left evidence of their liking for the prettier sex, and we hardly need mention the affairs of Louis XV, some of which had international repercussions. Now and then a chief of state goes further in his efforts to observe the tradition: Félix Faure, President of the Republic, was one, dying on the bed of honor in the arms of Meg Steinlen. In that affair a familiar comic note was sounded when a guard lost his way among the several meanings of the words meaning "to know." *"Le Président, a-t-il sa connaissance?"* (Is the President conscious?) asked the prefect who had hurried over upon receiving the grave news. *"Non,"* the guard replied, *"elle s'est enfuite par l'escalier de service"* (She took off by the service stairway).

Love in its sexual aspect is alive and well in French politics of the present day. Informed of the death of General de Gaulle, a lady in Roubaix cried out impulsively, "He is the only man I've been faithful to in the last thirty years." (*L'Express,* November 16, 1970.)

It sometimes seems that love hovers about the edges of life and influences it more in France than it does in other countries. In *The Sorrow and the Pity,* a documentary film recently shown in Paris and the United States, ex-premier Mendès-France related how he had escaped from the prison camp at Riom. Having scrambled to the top of the prison wall, he was about to jump for the street and liberty when a young couple stopped exactly beneath him. The young man was attempting to seduce his friend and she resisted. Mendès-France held on above, knowing that any second his flight might be discovered, and prayed—to the devil, of course—that she would give in and they would leave. The story, told lightly but never with poor taste, had a happy ending. The couple proceeded up the street, and Mendès-France observed: "That young man will never know, but my happiness that night was even greater than his own."

When the lewdness of public officials has been thoroughly ventilated, there always remain the affairs of our present-day kings, the movie stars, television personalities, and popular singers. In this field French gossip has found a tireless collaborator in the country's leading artist. By herself Brigitte Bardot could supply 20 per cent of the information that the French want to know about the binomial of love and sex. "B.B., proud to show off her newest love," proclaimed a caption in *Ici-Paris* (August 6, 1968; circulation, more than a million copies).

But Brigitte was only the first and most famous in a series of persons about whom that issue of the paper had the same sort of news to report. A crime of passion was found to be understandable because "Anne Marie liked to dance with Fesarn, but refused to let him have his way." "Six admirers of Christine Fábregas"—the contestants on a television program that she conducted. "I deceived Georgette Lemaire. Daniel never talked to me about anyone else. Daniel will always love her," confessed the artist's secretary. "Nicolette has found her first love again." "This leopard [photograph of an actress in a leopard-skin coat] is Lauren Bacall, madly in love with Humphrey Bogart." In other stories, the drama resided in the reaction of a child to a familiar situation. "Where is Papa?" the child asks, and the dramatic clarification follows: "Magali Noël doesn't want her son to know that her marriage is broken."

Breakups are almost always caused by infidelity. That's the English word for it, but the French use a verb that corresponds a little better to day-by-day, or rather night-by-night reality. In the same issue of *Ici-Paris,* the verb appears in a reader's letter to a lonely hearts column: *"Mon mari a découché." De-coucher* is to sleep somewhere else. The word *coucher* itself is used obsessively in the French language, both seriously and in jest. When someone asks how things are going, the French swinger doesn't say *"cosí, cosá"* but *"couchi-coucha."* With respect to the reader's problem, the column gave this advice: *"N'en faites pas un drame"* (Don't make a scene; it may be a trivial adventure and your husband might easily just come home of his own accord).

It is about the only response that many foreigners can imagine a French person giving. "Don't get hysterical over

LUST

something so simple, ordinary, and repetitious as marital infidelity." After all, the French . . . Spaniards who don't know another word of French nevertheless recognize the word *cocu* (cuckold), which they assume is a word like "guy" or some sort of nickname for a national from the other side of the Pyrenees.

Like many stable lines of discussion about particular countries, this one got going and continues with the help of the party interested. Not only do the French continually present the theme of infidelity in their plays and movies, they treat it as something normal. In the hit of the 1968–69 season, *La Facture,* the hero advises: "A happy marriage is not achieved by complete fidelity but by the partners having their affairs simultaneously." The trouble is, suggests the author Françoise Dorin, that infidelities get out of phase. That development seems unavoidable and its possibility casts a shadow over French marriages from the start.

Even when the married couple love and desire each other? Éléonore considers this question in Françoise Sagan's play *The Swedish Castle:* "When a woman has a husband she loves and still, out of some mental perversity, takes a lover besides, the lover has got to be a lighthearted, happy fellow; in that way the ridiculous person isn't her husband."

There is, in spite of everything, something ridiculous about infidelity. And it continues to be offensive. Obviously it would not appear so often as a problem on the stage and screen if it were as normal as some people think.

> A husband but no lover
> is a halfway measure.
>
> A. de Monteur, *La Comédie des proverbes,* 1616.

Possibly the need to have a lover is part of the folklore of life in France. It may be that many Frenchmen have mistresses or lovers to maintain France's reputation in history—that is, out of pure patriotism. In his recent book,

The Sexual Behavior of the Married Man in France, Jacques Baroche maintains that 90 per cent of the husbands he interviewed confessed that they had been unfaithful to their wives, but explained that the requirements of modern living had tended to replace steady arrangements with rapid adventures.

Not that one can't find plenty of strict, upright, old-fashioned husbands in France, especially in the provinces. The Spanish type who shoots down the man he thinks is his wife's lover is still around. The *France-Dimanche* of July 30, 1968, gave an entire page to a case of this kind. I will quote only the caption beneath the photograph: "Jeanine Pinchart was too beautiful for her husband, who suspected her, despite her constant protests of innocence. He could not believe that friendship was the only aim of Raymond Mathias. Still without any proof, one morning Pierre shot at Raymond."

(If marital infidelity were completely accepted, there would be less divorce. Who would need one? The statistics show that 11 per cent of French marriages end in divorce, and this figure rises to 17 per cent in the large cities.)

It seems evident that French society accepts very simply a relationship that in other countries is regarded as clandestine and even unmentionable. No one quibbles about calling a concubine "Madame," single though she may be, and when a journalist has occasion to mention a woman's irregular relationship, he is likely to write that she shot, or helped, or saved "her lover" with the same neutral emphasis that he would use to say "her husband."

It is regarded as equally natural that a man should have a mistress. When a gentleman of a certain age goes to buy a present, the salesgirl will suggest something for his *"petite amie"* without giving offense. Why shouldn't he have one?

One of the most beautiful sonnets in world literature was written by Ronsard to convince his beloved to yield to his importunities. After describing how she would look, grown old, sitting next to the fire and recalling that "Ronsard praised me when I was beautiful," he warns her that by then it will be too late, because he would already have become a ghost. The two final verses encourage her to enjoy the hours of her youth:

> *Vivez, si m'en croyez, n'attendez à demain*
> *Cueillez des aujourd'hui, les roses de la vie.*

> (Live, if you believe me, don't await tomorrow, gather up today the roses of your life.)

The verses are typical of the Renaissance and its repetition of the pagan theme of *carpe diem,* but in France they still seem contemporary. Life's roses are to be picked when one is young ... but then it can't be said either that one has to renounce them when he grows old.

In the following paragraphs, a French lady states her right to love. Her reasoning was devoured by the readers of *France-Dimanche* (January 27, 1970), a mass-circulation paper. The writer, a widow, tells of her sorrow after the death of her husband until one day, unexpectedly,

> I felt troubled by the glance of a passerby, and I realized that I was missing something—love. Not the spiritual kind of love, which continued to be united in my mind with the memory of my husband, but physical love, which my body, despite my faithfulness to my husband's memory, was demanding as insistently as it would have demanded bread if I were hungry, or water if I were thirsty.

The situation seemed simple: marry again. But no, because

> my children retained a fanatical admiration for their father. And besides, I couldn't myself imagine any man taking the place of the one I had lost.

There remained, then, just one solution, which *France-Dimanche* printed in capital letters:

> TAKE A LOVER. Lead a life with him parallel to my life with my family. I had made up my mind. I would give

another man a place in my life but not the one that Paul [the husband] had left.

But, how to tell the children? First to fourteen-year-old Françoise:

> We cried, remembering the father and husband we had lost, but in the end she said to me, "Mama, I want you to be happy." And in fact, when Jacques [the lover] arrived for lunch one Sunday, my children adopted him.

The lady kept up appearances, however. Jacques never slept in the house.

> and I refused to let him make love to me in my bedroom, because there is a natural respect that one must maintain toward one's children.

An interesting confession. And the likelihood that it was all the creation of a *France-Dimanche* staffer doesn't rob it of significance. It still shows what the French like to read about—love relationships arranged on the basis of calculation and reason.

Amour knows no social limits and none of age. If a venerable old man can and should aspire to having a *petite amie,* the same holds for a matron mellow in body and advanced in years. On my first visit to France I was shocked by a spectacle that I was to see many times again, a café owner perched on her stool in front of the cash register and alternating her counting of change and her "*merci, Madame,*" "*merci, Monsieur, au revoir, Messieurs-Dames*" with passionate glances at a robust, curly-headed youth eating voraciously at a table near her.

"It's her boy friend," explained the waitress without giving the matter any importance. On another occasion I was astonished to observe a respectable dowager, the owner of a hotel, making flagrantly seductive gestures at a young student passing by. "No," another waitress immediately assured me, "she would like to have a lover, but she doesn't dare because of the money it would cost her" (see Avarice).

LUST

When thirty-two-year-old Gabrielle Russier committed suicide a few years ago because the parents of her seventeen-year-old lover wouldn't let him go on seeing her, the French unanimously condemned the unsympathetic family.

It sometimes seems that a difference of ages in a relationship results from a search for variety rather than from any economic considerations. Françoise Sagan often uses the theme; in her first novel, *Bonjour, Tristesse,* the heroine's father has a mistress twenty years younger than himself. In her recent book *La Chamade,* a girl and boy are each united to a lover much older than they. Their attempt to throw off these yokes and to look for happiness where they logically might hope to find it, together in the commonality of their age and customs, fails badly. At the end of the book each returns to his old way of living.

A similar situation came to light recently in Marcelle Ségal's *Courrier du Coeur* column in the magazine *Elle.* A twenty-year-old girl had written in to ask whether her happiness could be as real as it seemed, given the fact that her lover was fifty-two. "Why shouldn't I believe that your happiness is genuine, Catalina," the columnist asked, "when you yourself give me the proof that it is?" To the girl's fear that her happiness might not be eternal, she responded: "Eternal happiness? It doesn't exist on earth, but a few years of happiness are always something to be thankful for. Let's not worry about a future that doesn't belong to us."

In her reply to the next letter, the columnist's sympathy seems even more inclusive. The reader had written: "Yesterday I telephoned to a friend who is divorced, just as I am myself. Her grandson answered, and asked me in surprise, 'But isn't my grandmother with you?' Once again my friend had used me as an alibi without bothering to tell me and had sunk herself in a tangle of lies to her grandson, who for his part sleeps with anyone he can. I don't agree. I also have a lover. My children know it and he is received in our house." The woman ended by asking Marcelle Ségal whether she thought it was good to lie to children in these matters. Naturally, the columnist replied that it was good for children to know that their mother is at the same time a woman (and clearly a woman with no thought of retirement).

No French woman, old as she may be, ever seems to resign herself to a stocking nightcap and loneliness. Here are some want ads from the matrimony section of *Ici-Paris:* "Seventy-three years old, *par.* sixty [which may mean she appears to be no more than sixty], slender, friendly, sweet, lithe, wishes to marry a gentleman." Another: "Fifty-five years old and wishes to marry to find happiness." The desire to find a happy life is expressed again by another woman who describes herself as "Fifty-eight; lives in Paris." A sixty-year-old widow from La Gironde is seeking a serious man to share her home. Two other women advise that they are widows with no children still at home, which seems reasonable considering that one is seventy-eight and the other seventy years old.

Sometimes the person placing the ad possesses an impressive list of qualities, such as, for example, the forty-eight-year-old widowed secretary with no children who assures us that she has "charm, elegance, a youthful look and personality, high morals and will surely make a gentleman happy who is between fifty and seventy."

The way French women cling to their illusions of youthfulness is shown by an ugly custom that clashes with their usual elegance and good taste. I am referring to the heavy makeup used by older ladies. Even Colette—intelligent, sensible Colette!—a woman of exquisite taste in her novels, put so much rouge on her cheeks that in her last years she looked as if she were wearing a mask. Many Colettes can be seen in France today, in the markets, the subways, and the buses. With their hair dyed bright yellow (not blonde), their eyes darkened by an overgenerous application of eye-liner, and spots of red applied to their cheeks, they seem a gross caricature of the traditionally *soignée* Frenchwoman, whose creams and dyes and thousands of

LUST

hours of primping can never be detected, only divined from their perfect result.

LOVE IN THE STREETS

> Hector: You like men.
> Helen: I don't hate them. It's pleasant to have them rubbing against me like giant bars of soap. One feels so clean....
>
> Jean Giraudoux, *Tiger at the Gates* (1935)

It's hard to exaggerate in talking about this subject. Love in Paris is out in the open for all to see. There are couples kissing each other on every corner, on foot, or in parked cars, high in the Eiffel Tower, or along the banks of the Seine, next to the hobo of the day. Kiosks showing flesh of every tone and tint to the city's international clientele, films overstepping the outer limits of audacity in every movie house, and naturally the sellers of old books on the river's quays: somehow even they manage to give their wares erotic overtones. The Seine would be just another river in any other city, a current of filthy water used as a highway by solemn gray cargo barges and now and then a tourist launch, one of the famous *bateaux-mouches* decorated with colored lights, flickering with the flashes of a hundred tourist cameras.

But in Paris the Seine is something else. Years ago a song was written—it is still remembered today—that endowed the river with sensualism:

> *Car la Seine est une amante*
> *et Paris dort dans son lit.*

Only the imagination of the French could have transformed this prosaic, much-dredged river into a bed for the battles of love.

LUST

Love is in the streets and also the hotels, where no distinction has been made for many years between married couples in from the provinces who wish to spend a few chaste nights, and lovebirds there for the afternoon. "Today everyone makes love in the afternoon," says one of Françoise Sagan's characters. "In the evening we're just too tired." Love is reflected in the design of French double beds, wide and generous in a country distinguished by the meanness of its furniture, especially its tables and chairs.

In other countries a concrete, social, visible difference exists between normal people and people who collaborate in the assignations of others. In France, particularly in Paris, no such distinction can be detected. The woman in charge of a small hotel in Spain or Italy who offers a room to a furtive couple has an unpleasant look of complicity. In France she is a respectable lady and rents rooms with the same expression—and the same suspicion that they may try to slip out without paying—to a pair of students from the Sorbonne as to a married couple from Bordeaux. You also encounter the type who surreptitiously offers you obscene photographs in the hollow of her hand, but what she is evading is not censure by public morality, just the rules of the police. If the wares presented are within the limits of the law—and the law is still relatively liberal in these matters though de Gaulle and Pompidou tightened things up a bit—the buyer hailing from the provinces or abroad is more embarrassed than the seller. The seller handles such products because people want to buy them, and with the proceeds he can set up a legitimate business.

Sometimes, of course, they do establish a limit, if only speculatively. I remember a conversation I had with a well-dressed, apparently bourgeois lady in front of her used-bookstand on one of the quays of the Seine. With a smiling face, the *chère madame* was exhibiting books with such fetching titles as *Summer Nights, The Worst Sin, Louise's Vacation, Scandalous Tales of the Convent.* I asked her how business was going. She informed me that some of her best-selling books were hidden because they couldn't be displayed. Citing an especially popular title that described lesbian relationships, she said matter of factly, "Everyone has his own tastes, Monsieur, but the truth is, these things don't seem normal to me."

A hotel offering "furnished rooms" is synonymous with a house of assignation in many countries, and Spaniards nudge each other with their elbows when they see such signs in French streets. But this supposed distinction between types of lodgings exists only in the superheated imagination of the visitor. Because the term *meublé,* "furnished," is simply an obsolete declaration of the type of hotel it is, and couples may in fact enter it to pass a few hours exactly as they may in any hotel that classifies itself in some other way.

> I made love to a woman from time to time. But first you have to please them, then undress them, then dress them, and finally displease them so they will let you leave. It's a lot of work.
>
> Jean Giraudoux, *Amphitryon 38.*

"For Anglo-Saxons, eroticism is a relief; for Frenchmen, it is a refinement." This was Eugene Ionesco's comment about the problem of adapting *Oh! Calcutta!* to the French stage. The play provided an example of what he meant. In the original version, a group of beautiful people drink champagne, admit their erotic fantasies, and fondle each other to illustrate them. In the version being shown in Paris, a similar group drinks champagne (what else?) but they don't go so far as to touch each other and their speeches are erotic masterpieces of impeccably literary descent—poems by Ronsard, Apollinaire, La Fontaine, Musset.

"The French nation," said a man who knew the country well, "is a woman, and one must continually speak to her senses. Otherwise her restless spirit frets her, her temperature rises, and she gets carried away." (Napoleon, on St. Helena.)

LUST

The amorous capacity of the Frenchman is mentioned often, but curiously this capacity seems more a matter of form than of sexual intensity. French discoveries in the field of physical love are concerned with variations rather than the theme itself. The French have supplied names and promoted various positions that amplify the repertoire in countries with less imagination. In this connection, a story has been circulating which tells of a Frenchman and a foreigner who are discussing the number of positions currently in use in sexual intercourse. The foreigner thinks there are ten, but the Frenchman believes there are only nine, and he is indignant that anyone abroad should presume to dispute such a matter with an expert. Faced with the foreigner's insistence, he challenges him to list them, and the foreigner begins: "Well, first, obviously, the woman lying face upward, the man stretched out on top of her, looking in her face. . . ."

"*Mon Dieu!*" exclaims the Frenchman, "that's true! That's one position I'd forgotten."

The French, masters of sauces in cooking, have also invented them for physical love. These sauces make love more interesting, but one is always tempted to suspect that they don't really improve the quality of the product so much as to hide its defects, as happens with steak. Many of the variations that we have mentioned before may be "in addition to," but in other cases they may be "in place of," allowing one to obtain the same result—and even the reputation of specialist—with a clear saving of physical force.

The most widely banned record in Europe these days is probably *"Je t'aime . . . moi non plus"* (I love you, I don't either). The moans, sighs, and broken exclamations on the disc reflect the labor, old as mankind, that a man and a woman are carrying to a conclusion. Its author, Serge Gainsbourg, explained the record's apparently poor sound quality. "We tried to give the listener the feeling that the scene is authentic and that it was recorded, sometimes not too well, by a tape recorder hidden under the bed." Thus the listener is thrilled even more, as if he were listening from a hiding place and imagining the scene.

In other cases the variation or prologue follows a deviate path to arrive at the principal object. The Marquis de Sade obviously required the auxiliary element of cruelty to reach the state that a Spanish peasant achieves by merely seeing an upturned skirt. Following this theory a little further, it may be that all the audio-visual materials that the French produce and that dazzle the foreigner—*cochon* (or filthy) movies, the pornographic postcards peddled by a man in a gabardine overcoat and furtive glance, the question "Do you want something special?" broached by the doorman at La Nouvelle Eve in the Place Pigalle if the photos of naked women in the window seem to leave you indifferent—these materials may all represent, not the luxuriant forms in which an excess of sensuality finds expression, but a series of injections that the average Frenchman must give himself to achieve his sexual goals.

If this were so, French *amour* would be, above all, an impressive exhibition of egotism. Sexual relations are sought not for the pleasure they may give another, but for one's own gratification. And if one must harm one's partner to obtain this personal pleasure, that's just too bad. De Sade's theory was essentially this, and in a milder form, it may be Françoise Sagan's philosophy as well:

"In him I had discovered the perfume of my own body. It is always on the bodies of others that one discovers one's own, its limits, its odor—at first with distrust, then with gratitude." This according to the protagonist of *A Certain Smile,* speaking of her first lover, Bernard. What Bernard enjoyed or suffered was secondary—the important thing was what she felt or thought herself. (Egotism is a strong trait in most of Sagan's female characters; they always do what they find convenient and amusing, not simply at the expense of local customs or morals, but to someone else's harm. From *Bonjour, Tristesse* to *La Chamade,* the protagonist—Sagan herself, one usually imagines—acts as

LUST

she pleases, no matter who gets hurt. The few moments of remorse recorded seem rooted more in masochistic pleasure than in genuine grief over anyone else's sorrow.)

Recent critics have sighted the glint of literary genius in de Sade, but his isn't the only case of intelligence placed at the service of an erotic system. France's greatest writers have sometimes shown their skills at describing carnal acts. They weren't trying to lower their writing to the level of sex, but to raise sexual matters to the level of the best literature. Alfred de Musset never was ashamed of his obscene novel *Gamiani,* and narrations of exceptional salacity recently have been attributed to writers of the first rank. The *History of O* was credited to a member of the Academy who died not long ago, Jean Paulhan; the scandal caused by the book was at best a minor one. If a book like that came out in Italy, Spain, England, or the United States, irate citizens would at once demand that the offender resign his official posts.

In some of these same countries it would be just as scandalous for an important woman writer to dedicate a book to the special relations of two women, and then to make an open confession of her own lesbian tendencies. I am referring to Violette Leduc. Jean Genet's stormy life—he's been thrown in jail several times as a sexual pervert—never prevented Sartre, among others, from acclaiming him as one of the geniuses of French literature. And Sartre himself passed from the philosophic speculation of *Being and Nothingness* to the almost obscene stories in *Nausea* without anyone in France feeling shocked. This attitude can be traced to two sources. The first is the incredibly high esteem accorded in France to intellectuals (see Pride), which permits the mandarin—the writer recognized and accepted as such—the greatest latitude in his themes. The second is the traditional French belief that things related to lust are one of life's constant realities and that it is only logical that they should appear in books, newspapers, and musical reviews.

In general, the French attitude toward homosexuality is

broad-minded. According to a survey taken by *Paris-Match* in February 1970, 49 per cent of the respondents thought that homosexuality should be tolerated, though discouraged; 19 per cent thought it would be best to forget that the problem existed; and only 29 per cent thought that it should be prohibited.

Inverts have often held a place of honor in French letters. The *jeunes filles* of Proust's *À l'ombre des jeunes filles en fleurs (Within a Budding Grove* is the English title) are said to really be young men, and critics have remarked how little emphasis Proust's descriptions give to the typically feminine parts of the bodies of his women characters—their breasts and hips, for example.

Jean Cocteau's special tastes have always been accepted without a ripple of scandal. André Gide's inversion is studied as a function of his work, in a literary, not an ethical or moral way. With equal objectivity critics study the influence of sexual appetite on a man who wrote with as superhuman a voraciousness as he loved, Victor Hugo.

HIS MAJESTY THE BIDET

According to recent statistics, 11 per cent of French houses are without running water, 53 per cent have no toilet, and 63 per cent don't have a shower. These figures suggest that sanitary conditions in France—and the hygiene of the people—leave much to be desired. Fortunately, the situation is not as bad as it seems because the absence of the facilities cited is partially compensated for by the presence of another, a utensil now the universally recognized symbol of the French nation, which in a photograph permits instant identification of the house as French. I refer to the bidet.

The bidet is in every bathroom in France and, when no bathroom exists, in the immense majority of the country's bedrooms. The humblest small-town inn may lack every convenience from heat to a light by the bed, but it will never be without the instrument an Aragonese peasant once defined in a bill of lading with unconscious wit as "a guitar-shaped object, use unknown."

The matter has gone so far that the bidet is now considered more vital than any other appliance. In a luxurious, brand-new hotel in Font-Romeu, a little town in the eastern French Pyrenees, the room that I was offered had no toilet but did have a bidet. They apparently reasoned that it was more logical to go out into the hall to use the former than the latter.

The bidet is not just present everywhere; its presence is everywhere ostentatious and defiant. In modest homes the washstand is often behind a small folding screen, but not its little brother. It seems to be the soul of the French home: it presides, directs, and perhaps makes you remember something. (And for the foreigner, especially the Anglo-Saxon, it seems so conspicuous that he doesn't know where to look when his eye lights on it during a visit to the house.)

Love in France is accepted like the air around us, with absolute naturalness. It has always been this way and the romantic history of the country, as we have seen, parallels and sometimes becomes entwined with its political history. *"Ça c'est naturel."* Lately, however, the French have begun to intellectualize love in a new way and turn it into a problem, following the example set by the Americans that we took note of in Pride. It's not that they are still trying to explain love's reasons, as French thinkers have been doing since the days of Pascal, but to account for sexual events by means of exact descriptions and deductions. The only books the French used to need were pornographic tomes that described with varying degrees of linguistic elegance certain physical occurrences, for the purpose of amusing and exciting the reader.

Today, however, a new type of publication has appeared

which attempts to investigate the reason for things happening the way they do. In the United States, with its history of puritanism, such books fill a genuine need, because the people have to approach physical matters scientifically if they are ever to convince themselves. But in France the new publications seem utterly useless, for the historical character of the people is frivolity itself. The Frenchman's sexual education is his environment and he doesn't have to look for it in scientific treatises.

A curious thing happened during the events of May 1968: couples made love in the traditional French style in the courtyards of the liberated buildings, but at the same time the students tried to put forward as a problem something that had never been one before. When the Minister of Youth, Missofle, visited the college at Nanterre (where the whole revolutionary movement started), Daniel Cohn-Bendit reproached him because his emergency *White Paper* on youth didn't contain a single line referring to sexuality. The minister's reply was what you'd expect from an old Gaul who couldn't comprehend why *that* should be the object of scientific inquiry: "If you have problems of that kind, no one is keeping you from diving in a swimming pool." It's worth remembering that Cohn-Bendit is German by birth.

"Good revolutionaries kiss each other at least once a night," said a poster on the Sorbonne (May 22, 1968), and another announced, "The more I want to make a revolution, the more I want to make love."

The magazine *Lui* is the French equivalent of *Playboy,* and it also attempts, between one nude photo and the next, to investigate the reason why the reader likes to see them. In the issue for October 1968 a specialist, Dr. Hennequin, explained that the magazine was needed by certain adolescents; it provided a release for those who only rarely felt any physical sensuality. But, the doctor continued, a magazine of this sort can make others desire what is not within reach, and this condition is dangerous if it continues for long. The solution he proposed was this: "I believe that desire is less intense if the text of the article makes the person looking at the photos reflect about sexuality and about what a woman can mean to a man. When a photograph that might otherwise be considered risqué, not licentious, induces reflection, I believe that we have a right and even a duty to make it available to everyone."

It's rather difficult for me to imagine a Spanish adolescent faced with a photograph of a scantily clad girl and an accompanying text meditating on the sociological importance of a woman in the life of a man. And I greatly fear that the same thing happens to French boys, no matter what Dr. Hennequin says, who is, after all, simply trying to carry an old French obsession, reflection and analysis, into the new territory of the mass media.

In the same Anglo-Saxon tradition of finding someone who doesn't know something and forcing everyone to learn it, a year or two ago some educators inaugurated a series of audio-visual sex education lectures in Paris. *France-Soir* recorded the comments of some of the high school students who attended the showings and heard the commentary of Dr. Jossay: "Only four positions!" "What a lack of imagination!" "But we knew all this already!"

> The heart has its reasons that reason doesn't know.
>
> Pascal.

The curious thing about the importance the French attach to *amour* is that it seems to contradict, in principle, the strongest support of their entire mental system, reason. Heart and head always fight for the will of man, and logically the former makes him lose his way. *"Folles amours font les gens bêtes"* ("Mad loves turn men into jackasses"), said François Villon in 1460, and Antoine Bret voiced the same thought in 1670: "The first sigh of love is the last of intelligence" *(L'École amoureuse).*

When Pascal said that the heart has reasons that reason doesn't know, he had encountered a way to restate the old duality that satisfied both the Cartesian mentality and the amorous longing of the average Frenchman. Thereafter, everyone felt easier about the dilemma. Although the Frenchman's motivations had now become plural, they were still all reasons, and he could maintain his reputation for thinking at every moment of his life. De Bonald, a century later, rang some more changes on the theme: "Great thoughts come from the heart and great results from the brain." From there it's a short step to Renan in the nineteenth century, who said, "Frivolous people are the only true wise men."

Yet there's no point in getting married thinking only about love; as Gabriel Meurier said, "When you marry for love, you will have good nights and bad days" (1568).

A joyous description of the act of love: "A gentle resistance, a gentle scuffle, and a gentle silence" (Giraudoux, *Amphitryon 38*).

A dramatically pessimistic description: "... What men and women call love, which consists in going to dark houses and to bedrooms sadder than they are themselves to unite in silence like shadows." (Henry de Montherlant, *Queen After Death.*)

Today the movie industry of almost every country has gone for nude scenes, but time was when only the French gave their films the spicy touch provided by the sight of feminine graces *au naturel.* In German and Czech films nudity was part of a message that tried to be profound and intellectual. The problem treated might be homosexuality in the schools *(Girls in Uniform)* or the sexual impotence of husbands *(Extasis),* but in French films no one needed to explain anything. A nude girl would come on the screen because to the director it seemed logical that she would appear that way in a film from his country, as if she were the movie's stamp of origin, the one detail necessary to make its nationality clear. So strong was this tendency that in many films, the nude has nothing whatever to do with the plot. A thief in flight, for example, might suddenly open a hallway door. "Ah!" exclaims a young woman struggling to cover a little of her body with a towel. Bang: the thief slams the door and hurries on his way. The plot of the movie also continues on its way, and the young lady is never mentioned again: her mission is over.

A journalist reported that he had been enchanted to see on the French television screen, for no apparent reason, "a superb young woman, naked as Eve coming from the hands of God." Anticipating that protests against the scene would be voiced by a few old maids, he hastened to build up a defense: "After so many war movies and scenes of horror, it is lovely to remember that we also have flowers and girls on this earth. Television informs, edifies, persuades, and distracts us, croons to us, and sometimes puts us to sleep, but it rarely surprises us. That brief sequence was no scandal. It is much more agreeable to see a girl naked than a government minister dressed." (*France-Soir,* January 25, 1970.)

France-Soir, a paper that boasts a circulation topping a million, also carries a short historical cartoon story in every issue—something like *Classic Comics.* Hundreds of people celebrated in this world for one thing or another have paraded through it. I don't remember ever seeing an issue in which at least one drawing didn't picture a young woman with a breast uncovered. The authors manage to get this sketch in even when they are treating the life of a monk canonized for his piety, because in this case they can show the monk having a sinful dream, or simply a vision of the scenes of perdition that he was destined to break up with his chaste example. It never failed. I imagine that the cartoonists, like movie directors, needed to stamp "made in France" on the newspaper page.

Tout est là, a caption proclaims at the bottom of a double-page spread in a recent issue of the family magazine *Paris-Match.* The *tout* in question is a collection of fifty photographs of feminine buttocks in different positions. Erotic advertising? A movie? A new review? Not at all. "Airborne," a chair manufacturer, just wants the public to know that it has its eye on its customer's welfare. "Our job consists of sitting down," the ad informs us, "anatomically, socially, and philosophically."

The first actresses of real importance to undress before the camera were probably French. Neither little Simone, in *Lake of Women,* nor Brigitte Bardot in *And God Created Woman,* Martine Carol in *Caroline,* Jeanne Moreau in *Lovers,* or Catherine Deneuve in *Belle de Jour* needed to undress to attract attention, as might be the case with less talented artists. The leading French stars just seem to believe that beauty should be shared by everyone. And their husbands agree. Roger Vadim, the movie director, is one of the most generous men in the world; no sooner does he marry some new beauty than he hastens to display her to millions of spectators, on giant screens if necessary. Why not? As the protagonist says in Anouilh's *Colombe,* "When I'm taking a bath and some man sees me through the front window, I let him look, poor fellow. Why shouldn't he enjoy himself?"

In the movies the French have Brigitte Bardot, direct, natural sexuality; Jeanne Moreau, twisted, malicious sexuality; and Catherine Deneuve, distant, mysterious sexuality.

And actors? They haven't caused as much of a sexual stir as the actresses, but sometimes even their ugliness—Aznavour, Montand, Belmondo—seems to transmit an erotic message.

"It's got to be true," Roger Vailland points out, "that women prefer Frenchmen. The extraordinary jealousy of their husbands forces you to believe it. Just look at an American when his wife is talking to a Frenchman." (He is exaggerating a little, though he may not know it. Americans are more jealous of Italians.)

Reasoning in France can explain everything. Because the Frenchman is a Cartesian. Descartes wrote the *Discourse on Method,* and every Frenchman thinks that he, too, possesses that kind of intellectual superiority as one of his principal characteristics. I heard a priest say it once, during a Mass in Saint Louis des Invalides: "... because we French are intelligent and Cartesian."

So what happens when a good session of reasoning has made everything clear? Anything can happen, even adultery. In *La Petite Hutte* (The Small Hut), a popular play by André Roussin, Philippe, his wife Suzanne, and her lover Henri—the classic French triangle—are cast ashore on a deserted island. The circumstances of the place now hamper the efforts of the lovers to see each other alone, as they had done in the big city, and therefore Henri decides to reveal everything to Philippe in the hopes that he will agree to share his wife with him. To the stupefied husband, he explains:

> Henri: You never suspected us and it became our obsession to keep things that way: it was a constant preoccupation that Suzanne and I had. Because true suffering, you know it as well as I do, comes from uncertainty and doubt. You didn't ever doubt us and I think you ought to thank us for that. Today, out of the clear blue sky, I've sprung the truth on you and it surprises you, paralyzes you for a moment, but it isn't something that need make you suffer. The reason I say you don't have to suffer is this: if you look this new truth squarely in the face and consider it calmly with the logical spirit that is so characteristic of you, you will quickly see that absolutely nothing has changed from the way it was in the past. Since we three were happy for six years, there isn't any reason why this happiness shouldn't continue. Tell me: are you suffering, Philippe?
>
> Philippe: I've been asking myself the same question. The fact that I am talking to you so naturally seems very odd to me.
>
> Henri: You see?

LUST

> Philippe: For the moment, you understand, I feel as if I had been anesthetized. . . . I feel as if I were in the water, or rather under water, and yet the water can't touch my skin—as if I were wearing a diving suit. And in fact I feel as if I weighed three hundred pounds.
>
> Henri: It's the shock. You've been shocked, naturally. That's normal. Walk around a little. Take some deep breaths.

Suzanne uses the same logic when she learns that her husband has found out everything.

> Philippe: You've been deceiving me for six years.
> Suzanne: Yes, sweet, what else could we do?
> Philippe: I wouldn't have believed it of you.
> Suzanne: I know. But "deceived" isn't the right word, darling. Because if we were literal about it, it would be equally correct to say that for six years I had been deceiving Henri with you.
> Philippe: That never would have occurred to me, either.
> Suzanne: And the things I have done for you that I never told you about!
> Philippe: What, for example?
> Suzanne: Thousands . . . make up an excuse to explain why the three of us couldn't go out somewhere, so that I could stay home and read a book at your side. I never read a book in bed with Henri; we saw each other only in the afternoons. Do you think we never wanted to take a trip together? But we never did, and as Henri rightly said, if you think it was bad faith that we deceived you for six years, from now on you can't say the same thing. Now there can't be anything offensive to you in our relationship.

Philippe, logical and Cartesian as ever, ends up understanding the situation and agreeing that his wife should spend alternate weeks with him and with Henri.

Sometimes the plot in French plays gets even more complicated and relationships start to involve incest. Bern-

LUST

stein was a master of this sort of drama, which led Tristán Bernard to satirize his works as follows:

"Have you seen Bernstein's new play? The plot is very exciting. A son is in love with his mother. But in the last act, thanks to some letters, he finds out that she's actually not his real mother at all, so in desperation he commits suicide."

Yes, the brain has got to keep functioning at all times. Otherwise there can't be any real pleasure.

"Tahiti is a paradise, but a paradise in which no one thinks. An intelligent hell is preferable to an animal paradise." (Victor Hugo, *Ninety-Three.*)

How curious that France, for so long the vanguard of sexual propaganda, should today have fallen so far behind. Symbolic of this newfound backwardness is the voluntary exile of Maurice Girodias, the editor of Olympia Press, who used to launch books in Paris that no one else dared to publish anywhere, including Henry Miller's two *Tropic*s and Vladimir Nabokov's *Lolita.* Today, Girodias has had to go back to the United States, once so straitlaced, which now permits (thanks to a series of circumstances that I examined in *The Seven Deadly Sins in the United States)* the publication of works prohibited in France, a country purified and transformed, to a certain extent, by General de Gaulle.

It's not just America, however. Even in Europe several countries now have more lavish offerings of obscene literature than France. Lately Denmark has seized the lead, authorizing magazines of every description, graphic as they might be. Actually, rather than authorizing anything, the country lifted its censorship, which had the same result. The publishers took care of the rest.

The French press has studied the scene in Denmark with great care. One correspondent, specially sent to cover the publishing phenomenon that developed with the ending of censorship, nostalgically concluded his report by saying, "These publications would be prohibited in France." One of the best-known myths about high life on this earth lay shattered. Paris, the "gay Paree" of Americans and Englishmen, the city radiant with a halo of naked women in the fiery imaginations of Italians, Spaniards, and Portuguese, whose eyes lit up at the very mention of a trip to the French capital, had been converted, erotically speaking, into a provincial city; the center of interest had passed to the capitals of the Scandinavian and English-speaking countries.

Not that the naked breast has been covered up. It continues to be the symbol of Paris, better remembered than the ship that appears on the great seal of the city. *"Tétons, toujours des tétons!"* exclaimed one Parisian, cloyed with them. All that has happened is that this exhibition of female flesh, so daring just a few years ago, has become almost a bourgeois entertainment compared to the sex spectaculars presented in British theaters, the advertisements on Swedish kiosks, or the female wrestling matches in the Sant Pauli section of Hamburg. It's not that France is offering less. The other countries are offering more.

Amour in France normally consists of sexual and romantic elements in equal parts, and the lack of either ingredient is enough to spoil the mixture.

A witty novel on this theme came out a few years ago. Maurice Bedel was its author and the title of the book, which won the Prix Goncourt, was *Jerome, Latitude 60 Degrees North*. It dealt with the life of a Frenchman in Oslo, a young fellow who was surprised and delighted to discover how liberated Norwegian women were in things sexual—especially appreciated by the Gaul—and social. More than once he found himself in a group of people who were getting along perfectly together and who were introduced to him more or less like this:

"This is my husband. That tall lady is the ex-wife of my husband, standing next to her new husband, formerly mine. And that's his daughter; she is talking with two men she was married to before. . . ."

The hero of the novel spends a few weeks in the country skiing, drinking, and above all vigorously making love. Until one day he decides to leave because he can't take it any more. His girl of the moment is surprised and hurt. "Don't you like it? Don't we get along perfectly? Don't you get what you want, when you want it, without problems?"

"That's why I'm leaving," exclaims the exasperated Frenchman, "precisely for that. I happen to like problems! I like to run into jealousy, resistance, and difficulties. I like passions, inconvenient as they may be."

Watching French authors ring the changes on the theme of love with their beautiful styles, one gets the impression at times that they enjoy writing about love as much as they enjoy carrying it out. In few literatures are there such delicate, exact, and beautiful examples of how love is born and develops.

In the first modern novel, Madame de La Fayette's *The Princess of Cleves,* two lovers discreetly confirm to each other the awakening of their mutual feelings with looks and expressions in the midst of a situation that is very difficult for them. In Stendhal's *The Red and the Black,* the protagonist, full of doubts and soliloquies, rationalizes his amorous behavior by making the conquest of a married woman a test of his own determination:

> One night Julien, gesticulating while he talked, touched Madame Rênal's hand. She drew it quickly away, but Julien thought that his duty consisted in attaining a situation in which her hand would not be withdrawn when he chose to touch it. The idea of a *duty* that he had to carry out and the notion that he would feel ridiculous or inferior if he failed to achieve it immediately dissipated all his happiness.

The night appointed for his adventure—for showing what he is capable of—at last arrives. Julien suffers in the darkness.

> The ferocious tension between his obligation and his timidity was too much for him. The clock sounded

> quarter to ten, without his having dared anything. Indignant at his own cowardice, Julien said to himself: "When the clock strikes ten I will do what I have been promising myself to do all day or I will go up to my room and blow out my brains."

When the moment arrives, Julien Sorel takes Madame Rênal's hand. At first she tries to resist but finally abandons herself to him. What she interpreted as a gesture of love was really only an intellectual move. When she in turn took the hand he had rested on the back of her chair, his immediate reaction was the experience of an electrical charge, not one racing over his skin, but in his brain.

> "This lady does not scorn me; that being the case, I've got to be sensitive to her beauty. I owe it to myself to become her lover."

Following the steps spelled out by his Cartesian logic, Julien Sorel, the tutor, becomes the intimate friend of the mother of his students.

The scientific yet beautiful explanation of the "crystallization" of love in another of Stendhal's works, *On Love,* is equally exquisite. André Maurois, whose *Climates* is an affecting study of the mysteries of jealousy, and Marcel Proust, are two more masters in the same French tradition.

When it comes to seeking love affairs to prove what one is capable of doing, few can rival Giacomo Casanova. Casanova was an Italian, but he wrote his book of *Memoirs* in French, and his mind and spirit are French also, for he was a typical gentleman of the eighteenth century. His long narrative portrays a man experiencing an incredible number of amorous successes, but successes that are always explained as a function of his superiority over other men. When he seduces a poor woman or a young girl—that is, someone inferior to him in age or social position—he has a very French way of teaching her something. Casanova wins over his women less with caresses than with technical words and observations about life and its

L U S T

pleasures. In his soul he is a pedagogue and at times he appears better pleased at having triumphed in dialectics than in later gathering the physical proof of his victory.

Frenchmen are inventive and some of the best locomotives in the world are French, as we all know, just as the Caravelle was the result of profound intelligence applied to the problems of flight. But not even in the field of pure technology can the French forget their obsession. In a curious book that appeared recently, *Brevets d'invention tout à fait insolites,* by Jacques Sée, we find, besides normal inventions meant to help men and women in their work or in the kitchen, others meant to improve the quality of their cohabitation—one, for example, that helps in the union of big women with little men. It's hard to imagine a citizen of any other country patiently dedicating his mental energies to solving a problem like that.

The interest of the French in sexual relations is not limited to humans. Thirty miles outside Paris the owner of an African-style zoo in which the animals roam freely about told some visiting newspapermen that the amorous record among his guests was held by a lion that had copulated seventy-four times with a lioness—the same one, he specified. When a skeptical reporter asked who had kept count, the owner, who responded to the Tartarinesque name of Paul de La Panouse, pointed to the guards. "They don't have much to do all day," he explained. *Time* magazine carried the notice of this exploit (June 14, 1971), but declined to vouch for its veracity, "even though the lions were French."

4 Anger

ANGER VS. REASON

Anger causes one to lose control. France is famous for its worship of reason. Reason is the opposite of losing control of oneself. Therefore, anger is rare in France.

Like so many others, this syllogism is false. Acts of anger occur in France just as much as anywhere else in the world, but the difference is that the French rationalize what they have done, so in their eyes it is justified. A Frenchman doesn't hit for the sake of hitting, like the citizens of more savage countries; he hits because the other fellow deserves it.

ANGER

Let's look at the record. Vauvenargues said, "Peace makes nations happy and men weak." This appears in his books *Réflexions* and *Maximes,* published in 1746. That is the eighteenth century, the Age of Reason, when Voltaire, Diderot, and Rousseau were denouncing brutality and violence, i.e., anger.

Remember *Candide.* The soldiers rape, kill, and destroy for the pure pleasure of doing so. Voltaire comments sarcastically about the official reasons given for their actions: country, religion, honor. How is it possible that people become so wicked?

A few years later we have the French Revolution, the direct descendant of the Encyclopedists, whose works exposed the stupidity of man when he takes justice into his own hands and the unjust violence that the upper classes wreak on the people beneath them. But the revolution showed that the lower classes can work violence on the people above them. The Terror sent thousands of citizens to the guillotine, some because they were enemies of the Republic, others because they *could* be her enemies. The Law of Suspects warned that persons were suspect "who by their conduct, relationships, words, or writings have shown themselves to be supporters of tyranny or federalism and enemies of liberty." Whether you supported Louis XVII or the Girondist republicans, it was all the same; the sentence was death in the new invention of Dr. Guillotin. Thousands were executed in the center of Paris, today called the Place de la Concorde.

Some time ago the historian Arnold Toynbee published a book in which he rejected the superficial and recurrent theory of a "yellow peril" to Europe and told of the many times that the contrary peril had existed in the history of civilization—times, that is, when the West had assaulted the East in search of gold, trade, or simply power. This type of revision could be worked with another European legend, the one that pictures poor France as the long-suffering and propitiatory victim of the expansionist yearnings of her neighbors. Since the year 800, when Charle-

ANGER

magne proclaimed himself Emperor of the West, until our own day, when de Gaulle worked for a Europe united from the Atlantic to the Urals, France has tried to be the queen of the continent. When she couldn't achieve that position by force, she attempted it by diplomacy, but she used arms to obtain it more times than most people remember.

In the modern epoch, French warring starts with Louis XII and Francis I, who disputed for control of Italy with the kings of Spain. When the Hapsburgs fell into decadence, no force remained in the West capable of resisting the French. Worms, Heidelberg, and Maestricht show traces of the power of French cannons from a time when the Sun King would travel in his enormous carriage to witness the siege of a city, and the city would be taken, while he watched, as a spectacle to entertain the ladies he had brought with him on the excursion. Between 1785 and 1813 the French invaded other countries fourteen times.

Law and reason, where were they then? Napoleon put an end to the assassinations of one band against another (hard as the republicans were on their enemies, we should not forget that the royalists of the Vendée were not all sweetness and light, either, in the way they treated republicans). The Corsican general unified the land. From the moment he took the reins of power, fresh from his triumphs in Egypt and Italy, the French stopped killing each other. From then on they dedicated their talents to killing foreigners.

The new French wave overran all Europe, this time armed with reason and modern logic. Napoleon inspired a new understanding in the old nations: the lay state, the abolition of feudal privileges, the end of the church's interference in the habits of the people. All this was summed up in the Napoleonic Code, the body of laws that eventually became the civil code for most of the countries of Europe.

Considering that France was the most advanced country, having seen the light before any of the others, it was only natural that she should rule throughout Europe. Only

A N G E R

backward and absurd countries refused to accept this self-evident truth, and Napoleon then had no choice but to kill the soldiers and peasants who denied it. Some were especially stubborn, first in Spain, then in Russia.

Napoleon was to die in exile, leaving behind a gigantic myth, very pleasing to Frenchmen of every political persuasion (see Pride), and fields full of bodies, including the bodies of his own followers, all over Europe. When the Emperor was told that 23,000 Frenchmen had died at Austerlitz, he is said to have commented, "Paris can make up the loss in one night."

More examples of violence? After the defeat of Napoleon III at Sedan, the Commune rose up in Paris and the rebellion was snuffed out with shrapnel. The pacifist Juarès was shot to death by a jingoist. In a period of seventy years, France entered three wars; defeated in all three, each time she was saved by her allies.

There are monuments in every town in France commemorating the Great War, the First World War. A much smaller number refer to the Resistance in the Second World War. The reason is clear. In the first contest, all Frenchmen fought against the Germans. In the second, the people were divided into friends and enemies, collaborationists and resisters. Much as the French now try to magnify the number and reputation of the latter group, the former still seem too numerous for that war to be a popular memory.

France's last three wars served to change her image. Circumstances probably had as much to do with this result as the skill with which the French always know how to take advantage of any break that comes along. In any case, France, set upon by the barbarians from the other side of the Rhine, no longer seemed the aggressor as in the time of Louis XIV or the Emperor Napoleon. Instead, she seemed the poor victim. Anger and violence were all on the other side.

I can't be completely sure about other countries, but in

ANGER

Spain this version of history has always surrounded us. In the first primer I was ever given to read, a story by Alphonse Daudet described the final class in the schoolhouse in a little Alsatian town. The Franco-Prussian War had ended and the occupying German troops had ordered the French schoolteacher out of town, so he could be replaced by a German. The dismissed teacher explained the situation to the students, and then proceeded to give the lesson of the day, which the students followed with unprecedented attention. At the end of the day, the teacher turned to the blackboard and wrote *Vive la France,* and I, who logically should have felt quite disinterested with respect to the problems on the Rhineland frontier, could hardly hold back my tears. The poor French!

The First World War was also always described to us in the same language of victims and aggressors. I remember how surprised I was in Innsbruck when I read the epitaph of an Austrian "fallen at Verdun." Until then, absurdly, I had thought that only Frenchmen had died on that field of battle.

But French violence didn't disappear simply because the violence of the Germans was greater. The occupation proved that. Thousands of people loyal to de Gaulle were tortured and murdered by Frenchmen working for the Gestapo. A few months later, thousands of other Frenchmen were tortured and murdered for having been loyal to Pétain. The Algerian war was another spectacle of cruelty.

Fortunately some people rebelled at all this bloodletting and spoke out publicly. After the Second World War they waited a while for passions to cool, but then they began to make their stand known against the violence committed by all sides. Later, when trouble arose in Algeria, the intellectuals, led by Jean-Paul Sartre, immediately declared their opposition to the government's policies. When someone suggested to de Gaulle that he ought to punish anyone who so clearly advocated high treason, the General answered, *"Sartre,*

ANGER

c'est aussi la France." A beautiful definition, sign of a military man's respect for a writer. But then let's not forget that de Gaulle was a writer, too.

(As these lines were being written, Sartre was challenging the French government to put him in jail as the director of an extreme leftist magazine. The government seemed determined not to please him, because it knew that his arrest would create a national uproar.)

Is there cruelty in the French soul? The country is so rationalistic that even an emotion as direct and primitive as the yearning for physical violence is premeditated and serves an intellectual end. The cruelty of the Marquis de Sade, for example, was at the service of sexual pleasure. The reason for the cruelty of the protagonists in Choderlos de Laclos's *Liaisons dangereuses,* also sadistic though not physical, was to do harm for the pleasure of doing so.

> "There are no more genuine passions in the nineteenth century," replied Altamira. "That's why one gets so bored in France. People commit the greatest cruelties, but without cruelty."
>
> "All the worse," said Julien; "when one commits a crime, he at least should do it with pleasure. Nothing else about a crime is any good, and on no other ground can one try to justify it even a little."
>
> Stendhal, *The Red and the Black,*
> Book II, Chapter 9.

In the last half-century or so the French theater has presented us with at least two characters who delight in cruelty as a substitute for other pleasures they can no longer indulge in at their age. The first is King Ferrante, a character in Henry de Montherlant's *Queen After Death.* "I have heard it said," he remarks in the third act, "that cruelty is the only pleasure left to an old man: in his soul it takes the place of the love that has disappeared."

The pleasure of making someone suffer is sought when

ANGER

one can't make them experience pleasure. The other character I remember in this connection is Demokos, the jingoist poet in Jean Giraudoux's *Tiger at the Gates*. He speaks like another impotent man, this time a man who lacks the capacity to go to war. "Since age keeps us out of combat," he advises, "let's at least do all we can to see that the combat is as cruel as possible." While Montherlant's King causes Inès to die, knowing she is innocent, Giraudoux's Demokos struggles mightily, even at the cost of lying, to make sure that the war of Troy will break out and his fellow men will die.

It's an interesting experiment to compare the local news that appears in the newspapers of two countries. I tried it and discovered that, while the Spanish papers report a series of violent deaths brought on by long-standing hatreds or by *machismo* ("they started arguing in a tavern and went out to the street to settle it"), the immense majority of deaths in the French papers are crimes of passion like those discussed in the chapter on Lust. Jealousy is almost always the key: it's the one emotion that makes the French forget *la raison,* the one obstacle that prevents them from determining their destiny on the basis of purely intellectual speculation.

The most notorious French crime of the last few years, one rich with startling revelations, was committed by a certain M. Dominici. The setting, a lonely country estate; Dominici's family in terror of his patriarchal manipulations of men and women, completely subject to his feudal discipline; the deaths of an entire British family touring the area, husband, wife, and daughter—all this produced a tremendous sensation. What could the motives have been? Dominici had money, there had been no disputes between him and the campers. . . .

It turned out that sex had reared its ugly head once more. Dominici, the old lecher, had slipped out into the night to watch the British couple undress through the little window in their house trailer. Surprised by the husband, he killed him, and then he finished off the wife and

ANGER

daughter to avoid being turned in. A horrible crime, in short, brought on by the caprice of a *voyeur,* another French word that has passed into many languages.

In their crime statistics of 1968, the police reported that the number of crimes attributable to sadism increased. *France-Soir* examined the figures, and its article gives a revealing glimpse of what the Frenchman considers normal and abnormal at the moment a crime is being committed. For example, the death of Maude Prin, a nineteen-year-old student who was killed not as a result of a tragic love affair but because someone was attempting to kidnap her in order to collect ransom. This crime the article considers abnormal. Further on, the writer speaks of Gerard Hubert having committed *"un crime stupide."* During an argument following an automobile crash, Hubert plunged a knife into M. Theodore. This violence hadn't been legitimized by any lover's passion and the paper qualified it with the harshest term that any Frenchman, the *homme de raison,* can apply to any act. Stupid.

Curiously, despite the increase in the population of France, the number of murders has been going down. Specifically, while there were 250 murders in the Paris region in 1938, there were only 230 in 1969. Holdups, on the other hand, increased 48 per cent between 1960 and 1968, and robberies involving violence rose from 136 in 1938 to 2,800 in 1968. Crime, it seems, is on the increase in France when there is a reason for it (see Avarice).

Usually, however, a contemporary Frenchman's anger seems to find expression in words rather than deeds. For his purpose he can draw on a wealth of words, and he combines and measures them out with the same skill that he exhibits in any other conversation. To hear a Frenchman of average education get mad is to receive a lesson in elegant speech. The reasons for his indignation are set out in perfectly logical order. His rage is so rhetorical that it eventually winds up a purely linguistic exercise, and as such it naturally loses its power to offend. To forestall this development, the Frenchman shores up his glittering phrases with expressions like *zut alors!* and, above all, the *ah, non!* which he says while rocking his head from side to side and curling his lips as if to say an "O." In English, his monologue would sound something like this:

"Well, if you think that I'm going to stay here all night waiting for you to make up your mind, *ah, non!*, you are very wrong, sir, wrong completely. I can't waste my time, sir; *ah, non!*, not in any way . . . and all this to earn a few francs; *ah, non!* If you want to do it, do it yourself, because we are not here to serve anyone; that would be good. *Ah, non! ah, non! AH, NON!*"

French anger grows greater the less justified it is. Let me explain. A man faced with a piece of work sometimes gets the idea that what he has to do is at odds with his self-esteem—an important emotion everywhere in the world, but especially in France. This is why French concierges, for example, are so terribly irritable. They know that their job is to be at the disposal of the tenants and of the visitors who ask for them, but this angers them, for they see it as a kind of servitude that they are not disposed to tolerate in their capacity as free and independent women. If the person who inquires is a foreigner, all the less so.

For this reason a person making an inquiry must be careful not to insinuate (he doesn't have to say anything, it's enough that his expression shows it) that he expects service from the person who is there expressly for this purpose. If he slips, a storm of harsh words may descend on him like an icy shower. He probably won't hear real swearing, and the sentences will be interrupted periodically by the word Monsieur, but the essence of the message will be clear enough. He has gone too far.

In many small French cities you are still likely to find the classic little hotel with a few rooms, ruled over by an older woman. This lady likes to sleep at night, which makes sense after her long day's work, but the obvious solution of installing a night clerk terrifies her, since it represents an additional expense. Instead, she goes to bed

ANGER

after telling the traveler to call her when he needs to by ringing at the gate. This night bell generally has symbolic value, but like all symbols, no one should attempt to treat it as he might some substantial, practical thing. The naïve traveler who decides, after driving all day on the highway, to stretch his legs a bit and see the city, finds out why when he returns. After ringing the bell again and again, the lady comes down in a wrapper, mad as a wet hen. For as long as the stranger takes to reach his room and lock himself in, he hears her indignant harangue about the lack of consideration shown by some persons.

My nephew and a friend of his—I told part of this story in the chapter on Pride, but it bears repeating—once arrived in a city at 4:00 A.M. Exhausted by their trip, they innocently rang the night bell of the hotel. The conversation that followed between the indignant lady who owned the hotel and the new arrivals went something like this:

"What kind of an hour is this to be ringing the bell? What do you want?"

"A room."

"At five in the morning?"

"Yes, of course, we're worn out."

"Well, this is no time to be going to bed. Go away!"

"But, do you have a room or not?"

"Yes, but I'm not giving it to you."

"May one ask why not? We will gladly pay the full twenty-four hours."

"That doesn't matter. This is no hour to be going to bed, and that's that."

With that she slammed the door in their faces and marched off growling to herself.

I feel quite sure that behind this indignation, completely disproportionate to the situation, there lurked a desire on the part of the proprietor to muffle the cries of her conscience, a conscience telling her it is really no more than reasonable that a hotel should admit guests who want a room whenever they may arrive. An even graver consideration involved, the most provoking of all, was the idea that her attitude was costing her money (see Avarice).

ANGER

(Some provincial hotels remind the traveler while he is registering that should he return to the hotel after midnight, he will have to sleep in the street. And this is said with complete tranquillity, as a normal communication.)

In everyday life the anger of the French shows up in traffic more than anywhere else. You've got to see the gestures they make at each other when the noise or distance rules out voice communication. They smack their foreheads to indicate that the other fellow is crazy, they make the sign of the cornuto (one more reason to believe that adultery is not as normal in France as some foreigners think, or it wouldn't be an insult). Sometimes they jump out and run up to tell off a driver stalled in traffic who has pulled a "fishtail" on them—the maneuver of leaping ahead into another lane and leaving the lane he was in before blocked with the tail end of his car. As a general rule, the language of lady drivers is as violent as their husbands'.

What moral feelings do the French have about violence? Talleyrand used a chilling phrase when he learned that the Duke of Enghien had been shot on orders from Napoleon: "It's worse than a crime," he said; "it's an error." The sentiment is symbolic of a people who have placed the intellect far above ethical considerations.

French society is very friendly to animals. To understand this you need only observe the way they treat their dogs, which enter any restaurant and shove their snouts into their owners' plates and those of nearby patrons. The easiest—sometimes the only—way to make a French man or woman smile is to praise the pet he or she has along. I have mentioned in Lust that this affection doesn't end with the pet's death, since they go into mourning for him, if only in their hearts.

The Society for the Protection of Animals has considerable power in France, and the law severely punishes anyone who mistreats an animal. Tradition still permits bullfights in the south of France (this is one of the few instances in which the provinces have evaded the laws of

Paris), but this ancient custom continues to hurt the conscience of many Frenchmen.

Any injury caused to an animal produces a great impression. *France-Soir* reported (January 30, 1969) that a judge had condemned a man to ten days in jail for having thrown a cat out the window. The accused maintained that the animal, possessed by suicidal tendencies, had thrown itself out voluntarily, but the magistrate noted that cats almost always land on their feet, whereas this cat had landed on its back because it had been struck by the accused before it fell.

Sadly enough, all this love for animals disappears when the French discover a new taste that they can achieve by mistreating one of God's creatures, forcing its body to develop in some abnormal way so that its flesh will be better to eat.

The ortolan is one example: he is a little bunting that they keep in a tiny cage, to prevent him from exercising in the slightest way while they feed him profusely until his flesh is extremely tasty. A more famous example is the *foie-gras* industry. The movie *Mondo Cane* has a scene in which sinister-looking women are stuffing enormous quantities of food down the throats of a great many geese. The geese are tied and their beaks have been pried open with funnels. In a world full of hungry people and even hungrier animals who desperately hunt for the scraps that humans have discarded as inedible, French geese are condemned to eat without stopping, a form of torture that ends only with their death. Then the livers of these animals, hypertrophied by all the excess food they have eaten and by their inability to exercise, are made into a morsel that causes gourmets to shiver with pleasure, especially, of course, in France. "There's no place like France for producing dishes like these." No place, that is, where a sensual objective is reached at the cost of such suffering to helpless animals.

Apparently the French were also the ones who discovered that lobsters taste better when they are cooked alive,

ANGER

thrown into the boiling water while still moving. They seem almost surprised, the experts say, and their meat doesn't suffer the alteration that happens to lobsters cooked after they are dead.

(The day that St. Peter retires and passes the gatekeeper's job on to St. Francis of Assisi, not another Frenchman will get into heaven.)

Another torture suffered by animals in France—no less sadistic for being bloodless—was described by a reporter sent specially to Cahors to attend the annual convention of the *Docte collège des maîtres de la table* and the *Confrérie des frères en gueule,* groups whose names can be roughly translated as the Learned Society of Masters of the Table and the Fraternity of Friends of Good Eating. The highlight of the convention was a hunt for truffles with the help of the best guide available for the work, a hog. Tied to a rope leash, he sniffs around the base of oak trees looking for truffles; when he finds one, he digs it up with his snout, naturally with a strong desire to eat it immediately. This result is forestalled by the other members of the party, who yank on his rope and shower him with kicks while they gather up the booty (worth about $10 a pound). In the hunt covered by the reporter from the capital, the hog managed to turn up twenty truffles in half an hour (over two pounds), and of course didn't get to taste one of them. Were animals able to die of frustration, this fellow would have been a sure candidate.

France is the only country in Western Europe, besides Spain, that still has the death penalty, and it continues to carry it out with the sinister guillotine, named for its inventor, a Dr. Guillotin who assured everyone that his idea had humanized capital punishment.

An anonymous contemporary muse satirized the invention as follows:

> *Monsieur Guillotin*
> *ce grand médicin*

ANGER

> *que l'amour du prochain*
> *occupe sans fin*
> *. . . prend la parole enfin.*
> *". . . En rêvant à la sourdine*
> *j'ai fait une machine*
> *qui met les têtes à bas.*
> *. . . Une certain ressort caché*
> *tout à coup étant lâché*
> *fait tomber, ber, ber*
> *fait sauter, ter, ter*
> *fait tomber,*
> *fait sauter,*
> *fait voler la tête . . .*
> *C'est bien plus honnête."*

Freely translated, this might go: "Monsieur Guillotin, a doctor so keen, neglecting no labor for love of his neighbor, finally begins to speak: 'Working unseen, I've made a machine that clips people's heads. A cute hidden spring, when tripped by a string, lets fall-al-al, lets drop-pop-pop, lets fall, lets drop, lets pop off a head. It's so very neat.'"

French cruelty is almost always practiced as reasonably as possible. We are back once again to the national obsession. No one, or practically no one, kills for the sake of killing—a trait worthy only of primitive, uncultured peoples—or because he can't stand someone or someone tramps on him in the subway. When a Frenchman kills he has his reasons, precise and egotistical ones, for doing it.

We have often referred to one of the cruelest men that France or indeed the world has ever known, the Marquis de Sade. He tortured and even killed because he derived sexual satisfaction from doing so: the pain and agony of others brought him pleasant sensations. His actions were a combination of pride (neither God nor the king had any business prohibiting whatever satisfied him), lust, and cruelty, an offshoot of anger.

ANGER

Three deadly sins for a single sinner. Someone else in French history, however, went him one better, adding to de Sade's three sins still another, this one the landmark of the country. The sin was avarice, the delinquent, Landru.

Like de Sade, Landru was intelligent, refined, and considered himself above the law, both human and divine, when he had a plan that he wanted to carry out. He didn't enjoy cruelty for its own sake, however, as had his predecessor in the eighteenth century. Landru regularly employed cruelty in his transactions because without it he would not have been able to realize his great dream: to get rich. De Sade used cruelty for the purposes of lust. Landru used lust and cruelty for the purposes of avarice.

Landru's adventures are typically French. The women he tempted were of diverse ages—we have already seen that French women observe no age limit in their aspirations for love—and to all of them he offered the hope of seeing realized a dream of their own, this one, too, very French, of having a little house in the suburbs of Paris. They all got into their little house all right, but they left it converted into smoke, by way of the chimney. Landru wasn't handsome or even good looking, but he had something that was even more important: he was interesting, gentle, and refined, and he played upon the romanticism of his solitude (he passed himself off as a widower) and his obvious culture at one and the same time. The combination was irresistible. Once a woman was infatuated with him, he got money from her in various ways, all of them ingenious, and then bought two tickets to go to the country—one round-trip, the other one-way. This incredible display of common sense was to damage him badly. A man this avaricious for the fortunes of his women was too French to bring himself to spend the little extra needed to buy round-trip tickets for his intended victims. "But they weren't going to use them! It would have been a shame," he

A N G E R

would have said. The ticket taker at the station, surprised by a detail repeated so often, was one of the prosecution's witnesses.

Pride, avarice, lust, anger—in truth, Landru combined a healthy collection of sins in one person and one situation. We can't tell to what extent he was influenced by a desire to satisfy his gluttony or whether envy drove him to crime, for he wanted to be as rich as other men. But it does seem clear that sloth never slowed him down. He was a hard worker.

5 Gluttony

EATING FOR PLEASURE

"Une dîner sans façon est une perfidie," wrote J. Berchoux, author of *La Gastronomie,* in 1802. A dinner without artistry is a fraud. No meal should be carelessly thrown together: one must fuss over it, manage it, enjoy it, and talk about it. The French have carried cooking to its highest pinnacles, and the peoples of the world know it. An American who wants to refer to something more elegant than normal American "cooking" uses the French word *cuisine,* and he would regard having a French cook in his home as a badge of great social distinction. Restau-

rants in the United States boast of their chef and their maître d' *(maître d'hôtel)*, and society people who are really *au courant* can distinguish between a gourmet and a gourmand. Other countries know these French terms as well as America.

The pride the French take in their own good cooking is shown by their attitude toward the cooking of their neighbors. The English, they think, eat everything half raw, the Germans only understand potatoes, the Italians eat spaghetti, and the Spaniards drown themselves in bad oil. Spanish cooking oil is constantly spoken of in France as a vile ingredient. I encountered the following passage in D'Appert's book *One Hundred Years of French History:* "The painter Manet fled to Spain. Despite his love for Goya, he couldn't bear to stay. All that cooking in oil drove him out." Perhaps a foreigner might be surprised to hear that local cooking could be more important to a painter than the paintings of the deaf immortal, but I'm sure every Frenchman would understand Manet's feelings. Cooking in oil. *Quels sauvages!*

The self-confidence of the French about their cooking shows up again and again. When I crossed the Atlantic in the *France,* I frequently praised the menu (the captain's dinner, offered on every voyage, is the best meal that I remember in my many years of touring the world of gastronomy), and the answer of my traveling companions was always the same: "What else could you expect on a French ship?"

The French live for, by, with, and on their cooking. The newspapers carry suggested menus every day, and they describe the courses eaten at official banquets so precisely that one sees clearly how very much the writers care for the art which is really the pride of their country.

According to *L'Express* of October 12, 1970, the Frenchman spends 43 per cent of his income on food and tobacco. He devours about 190 pounds of meat, more than the average American.

The butcher, the baker, and the pastry cook are regarded

GLUTTONY

as personal friends by the majority of the French; both men and women confer with them every day about the supremely important problem of how to feed their families. The personal, family quality of these relationships was highlighted a year or so ago when 160 Parisian butchers toured the great stockyards and packing plants in the United States. The butchers were moved by the huge factory workrooms that they saw, and by the incredible number of animals, all fattened exactly the same way on identical feed, from which precisely the same cuts were taken to be wrapped in cellophane and sent to every corner of the nation. They shook their heads in doubt.

"With us it is an art. Here it is technology. Many of us studied three years in the Écoles Supérieures des Métiers de la Viande. When I cut a piece of meat for someone we discuss who it's for, his father, his sister . . ."

The Americans reminded them that this sort of craftsmanship was disappearing, that American-style supermarkets were spreading around the world, even in Paris, and that their job was dying.

"Never," affirmed Jean Gibert, president of the Paris butchers' union. "We will never disappear so long as the Frenchman continues to enjoy a good glass of wine and a piece of cheese." (*International Herald Tribune,* August 11, 1970.)

Yes, the Frenchman eats with pleasure, and slowly. And when he finishes eating he begins to worry about the consequences. Because a meal that tastes good is usually a meal rich in calories and cholesterol. Accordingly, when the French stop talking about the pleasures of eating and drinking well, they start talking about the pain it causes them. "It is a vexing problem trying to conserve one's health with an excessive regimen," lamented La Rochefoucauld in his *Reflections.* But "no one is as happy as a glutton," affirms Rousseau.

And therefore the French prefer to eat all they want so they can enjoy repenting later. "Sin, repent, and sin again," is a Spanish saying. This is what the French do, but in terms of the fifth, not the third, deadly sin. And their penance is called Evian or Vichy, towns where they take the curing waters a few weeks every year, to redeem their past excesses and to permit them to commit some more.

Except in America, where nobody would dream of watching a movie without noisily chomping on popcorn, I've never seen moviegoers in any country as voracious as the French when they spot a candy seller's sign at intermission. *"Demandez le chocolat!"* the sign says, and they do ask for it, without paying much attention to standing in line. Candies of every sort rapidly vanish into the mouths of old people and children alike.

The French talk more about their liver—that victim of good food—than they talk about their hearts. The unfriendliest of taxi drivers (to pick a group in which the title for unfriendliness is the subject of stiff competition) will cheer up if you mention that your side aches a few minutes after you get in the cab. He will immediately tell you not only his own problems of this kind, but the symptoms of all his friends.

Vichy, in the minds of the French, is like a purgatory visited by those who have already been in paradise. The Second World War and the Occupation made the name Vichy more odious still. Pétain set up his government there and attempted to purge France of all her sins with a moralistic and frugal government. That's all he needed. The French were less able to pardon him this endeavor than his collaboration with the Germans.

The ability to eat well without suffering for it afterward would probably be the wish the majority of Frenchmen would choose to have granted, if heaven allowed them just one wish in all their life. "A good stomach and a bad heart are the secret of living a long life," said Fontenelle, who perhaps demonstrated the truth of his maxim by living for more than a hundred years (1656–1757). I doubt that all Frenchmen would accept this disjunctive, but if they couldn't get out of choosing . . .

GLUTTONY

Many countries have proverbs to the effect that the happiest husbands are not the ones who are loved the most but the best fed. The French, who have proverbs at hand to sum up any anecdote, have given their version of this one an elegant literary form: "The torch of love," their version goes, "is lighted in the kitchen."

The verbal opulence that helps the French sell their products is an aid in their kitchens as well. It's not just a matter of creating degrees like the *cordon bleu* or making sure that the immense majority of elegant dishes throughout the world have French names. Even the format of their menus seems to contain an implicit admonition, warning us: "This is a serious undertaking. You must try to approach these dishes as if they were religious objects, and conduct yourself while in this restaurant as if it were a temple. Now read what we are offering you."

The dishes follow, almost all of them delicious, well cooked, and elegantly presented. This is, of course, how it seems to the client, who is to a certain extent won over already by the world fame of French cooking, especially if he is a visitor from abroad. It suddenly occurred to me in one restaurant in Paris that French dishes are made to seem more impressive than the same food in other countries by simply listing them on the menu with an article or possessive pronoun—a trick that gives them a kind of hauteur they would never know in any other country. Inspired by this insight, I had sufficient patience to copy down the menu. Here it is:

Nos rôtis—nos légumes
Le roastbeef
Le gigot d'agneau
Le rôti de porc
Notre formidable plat de choucroute spéciale
    au champagne
Notre délicieuse soupe à l'oignon

GLUTTONY

Les nouilles fraîches
Les haricots verts
Les tomates provençales

Let's admit it, this creates quite an effect. Each dish has its adjective, or if not that, at least its place of origin, which seems like another adjective. Nobody but a Frenchman could have written it. Can you imagine a restaurant in any other country with a menu like this?

> Our roasts—our vegetables
> The roast beef
> The leg of lamb
> The roast pork
> Our magnificent dish of sauerkraut specially
>   made with champagne
> Our delicious onion soup
> The noodles, cooked to order
> The green beans
> The tomatoes from Provence

I doubt that any Spanish restaurateur would dare print a menu like this and expose himself to the "ah-hems" and "well-wells" of his clients.

To make a good meal you need, as everyone knows, a lot of skill, fine ingredients, and plenty of time. The French have developed and maintained the first, and they can still get the second if they are willing to pay enough, but as for the third, they are as short on time as any other people. To state the matter another way, time has become so expensive that they can't use it as generously as they once did. The arrival of a horde of strangers so absolutely lacking in gourmet exigencies as the Americans—Americans from both continents, since those from Caracas know as little about culinary refinements as those from Texas, Cleveland, or New York—has ended by disrupting the *cuisine* of France.

Look what has happened to the *bistro:* one ate well there

GLUTTONY

because the *patronne* was out back, as if to put her signature on every dish, and would appear at the end of every evening, inevitably fat and usually mustachioed, to receive the greetings of her old customers. Now the *patronne* has given way to a machine-like woman who brings out dishes at high speed to earn more money in less time. The intention was to imitate the American cafeteria, but the result is a hybrid. The new French establishments, particularly those in Paris, have sacrificed the sauces of old without achieving the hygiene or the style of hamburger known in the United States.

A good neighborhood restaurant, once found everywhere, now must be hunted for with determination, and people who know of one give the address only to their closest friends, so as not to destroy the goose that lays the golden eggs with an invasion of customers sure to result in the quick expansion and mechanization of the business. Except for a few of these treasured places, most tend toward the mediocre, and hundreds have brought down from a happier past only their name.

These are the worst of all. They always look nice enough on the surface. Dressed in a tuxedo, the maître d' has a solemn, patrician air as he shows you to your table and hands you your menu. The crystal is faultless, the tablecloths elegant. It promises to be a very good restaurant.

Until the food arrives. And then it becomes clear that the cook hasn't done well at all. Of the ancient tradition nothing remains except the shell—the attitude of the maître d', who continues to relive the glories of the past, and who furthermore refuses to accept, as a matter of principle, that a foreigner has any right to criticize something as delicate, subtle, and beyond his reach as French *cuisine*.

My most recent experience of this sort occurred only a few months ago in a restaurant in the Boulevard de la Madeleine. It was one of those restaurants with a café up front and tables for meals in the back, on a slightly higher level. Everything was solemn, glacially slow, and expensive. And the meat was tough.

GLUTTONY

"This meat is tough, maître."

He assumed an attitude that was a mixture of skepticism and boredom—how could that be? I insisted. He came up and looked at the meat. Finally he gave me a technical explanation.

"The meat is fresh, Monsieur, and for this reason it seems a little less tender."

"But I didn't ask for fresh meat. I asked for tender meat."

I have had many experiences like this in second-class restaurants. The fact is, while years ago one could eat extremely well in many places in Paris, now you can do so only in the exceptional neighborhood restaurants mentioned before, whose number is diminishing, and in the great luxury restaurants.

In these luxury establishments one still dines marvelously well, though their prices put their magic beyond the reach of anyone but persons who, in addition to being wealthy, come from countries with strong currencies. Thanks to these limitations, gluttony has won some adepts that it never had before. Because the elites of the world, particularly in the United States, are busy Europeanizing themselves just as rapidly as Europe is being Americanized. While the French talk about week ends, blue jeans, and martinis, the Americans are trying harder and harder to learn how to eat and drink like the French. I reported in my book *The Seven Deadly Sins in the United States* that this preference is purely literary and that, because of the difficulty of rapidly training the taste buds to discern new flavors, Uncle Sam's subjects often carry in their wallets the *Herald Tribune*'s list of Parisian restaurants with the best dishes served at each, and a card stating the best vintage years for each major wine.

Refinement usually succeeds comfort, just as comfort is pursued once the basic necessities of life have been acquired. Someone who has a comfortable house, warm in winter and cool in summer, and a diet that satisfies him physically, immediately starts looking for superfluous

GLUTTONY

delicacies—caviar, wines from the great vineyards, a Degas on the wall—in an ascending pattern that is repeated in every latitude. This makes me think that the pessimists who mourn the passing of great French cooking are wrong. True, its practitioners have been reduced to catering to a special type of customer, but these customers are becoming more numerous every day. They also come from every part of the world.

Meanwhile, most Frenchmen who eat out, like the great majority of foreigners who lack the resources necessary to visit the Tour d'Argent, will have to settle for a dish that is becoming more and more common and less and less appetizing—a dish that fills without pleasing, and that is, in truth, unworthy of the nation that invented international *haute cuisine.* I refer to the "French fries" (ironically, the American name for them has come all too true) that cover every plate in today's restaurants, taking space away from the meat, fish, and everything good that the country produces.

Another problem. If we took away champagne (it would be a mistake to do so, clearly) the French would be without a decent apéritif of their own. The best they have—pastis, Pernod, and absinthe—are poor in quality and more responsible than wine for the alcoholism in the country. So, despite their chauvinism, the French turn to foreign drinks—Scotch whisky, the American martini, dry Spanish sherry, Italian Carpano—to begin a meal.

Liqueurs for ending a meal, however, the French do have. Starting with cognac, soft as a caress, the repertory of liqueurs invented by the good monks of the country—Chartreuse, Cointreau, and the lady nearly as famous as the *veuve* Clicquot, Marie Brizard—is ample enough for anyone.

But we have skipped over what seems to me the deepest pothole in the otherwise smooth course of a French dinner—I mean their coffee. It seems quite unbelievable that the French have been so slow to learn that there is no such thing as a perfect dinner without the finishing touch of a cup of fine coffee. They recognize it themselves, I suspect. "The coffee here is pretty bad, the French charge," began an ad in *Paris-Match*. "While our country is world famous for the quality of its wines and the excellence of its cooking, we have to recognize this sad truth: French coffee is almost never any good."

The advertiser was a coffee company that thought it had found the solution to the problem. Nothing else could have explained the accusatory tone of the ad, because I have never met a single Frenchman who would admit that the coffee served in his country was unsatisfactory. How could anything made by the French be bad? When I once asked for coffee in a café in the rue Saint-Honoré, a woman took a half-filled pot off a shelf and put it on the burner.

"Madame, what are you doing? Are you going to give me reheated coffee?"

Her reply was completely French. She didn't tell me, "It's all we have; I'm sorry if you don't like it," or "I'll make some fresh for you." On the contrary.

"But that's how coffee is made!"

For many years French cafés served coffee in pots to natives and tourists alike. Then a few refined customers began demanding *filtre*, coffee made in the cup at your table. It took a frustratingly long time to pass through the filter, it tasted watery when it finally was ready, and I always burned my fingers when I tried to remove the top of the apparatus. Later, little by little (starting in the Avenue de l'Opéra, I believe), espresso machines were introduced and still the coffee they produced contained too much water.

France's difficulty in making good coffee can probably be traced to the fact that it is the only constituent of a French meal that is not native to the country. The French owe much of their culinary *savoir-faire* to careful preparation but even more to Mother Nature, who has been so lavish with her gastronomic gifts to them. The oysters on their coasts, the trout and salmon in their rivers, the abundant green pastures that feed their cattle and thus supply

GLUTTONY

them with meat, milk, and incredibly good cheeses, the truffles rooted up by the snouts of their pigs, the vineyards that produce the wherewithal to quench one's thirst while eating—the country has provided everything. Coffee is the only product that is foreign, or better, exotic. Other nationalities faced by a situation like this shrug their shoulders and simply make a national custom of whatever it is that they like from abroad. This is what the English did with the tea of India and what the Spanish did with chocolate from America. The best coffee in the world is probably served in Italy, where not a single ounce of the substance is grown and nobody can live without it.

But the Frenchman has difficulty believing that anything for the table can be made better somewhere else.

More or less as a footnote here, I might mention that the French import a lot of oysters from Spain, but in exchange they send back all their *anguilles.* This seems a grave lapse in their taste for good food, but I suppose their blindness is because eels are prepared with oil, an element that is completely taboo in French cuisine.

French society has achieved a radical transvaluation of values. Other countries worry all day long about their mining and agriculture, industries that the government pampers and helps. Simultaneously, but on a lesser plane, daily life goes on with all its frivolities: eating, drinking, dressing.

In France, other people's frivolities have become the nation's industry, mining, agriculture: the most important resource the French now have. Fashion designs are protected by law and anyone who attempts to copy a new dress goes to jail. The vineyards are regulated just as severely and anyone who places the words *appellation contrôle* on a label without official authorization is fined. There are years that never appear on bottle labels because the wine produced does not achieve a high enough grade or quality to merit listing. And so the bottles remain nameless at the back of the shelf, the subject of as much shame as if they

GLUTTONY

were illegitimate children, or, worse, retarded children in a bright family who are never mentioned in conversation.

It seems a dramatic and cruel way to deal with a less than perfect crop, something like the practice of the Spartans who threw sickly and deformed babies from Mount Taygetus, but it is really the only way to keep up a reputation for perfection.

The same thing happens with cooking. The high court of French restaurants is the *Guide Michelin,* a book published annually and which awards stars—those old-fashioned good conduct badges—to the restaurants that have earned them during the past year. And just as teachers recognize a new head of the class when the old one has been surpassed, so restaurants with four stars can suddenly lose one, or even two, in very grave cases, to make room for others that have improved.

As the scheduled publication date for a new edition of the *Guide* approaches, chefs begin to tremble and restaurant owners can't sleep. The Michelin envoys arrive without warning, sit down, and order a regular meal like any other customer. Only when they have finished eating do they identify themselves and ask to visit the kitchen, where they are taken by the proprietor himself, nearly overcome with emotion. After a careful inspection, they write a few notes in their books and leave. The owners can only pray that the impression they made was a good one and that they will at least receive the same rating as last year, if not rise to the next level. Their pride and naturally their greed are involved, because many tourists who don't know the gastronomical territory they are in drive through small towns looking for stars on restaurant façades before deciding where to eat.

In a town with a three-star restaurant, such tourists won't go to a place with just two stars, though this would be their choice as against a restaurant with only a single star or none at all. The door with no heraldic badge at all is as sad as any soldier without even a corporal's stripes.

GLUTTONY

The French didn't invent just a great *cuisine*. They also know how to complement it better than anyone else with wines and they serve it with perfect style and grace. From the way they set the table to the way they serve dessert, they know how best to conserve the heat, or coolness, or icy quality of each course.

I once heard a revealing and very French anecdote in this connection. In the course of an elegant formal dinner, one of the guests, a lady with an exceedingly low neckline, made a sudden gesture with such bad luck that one of her breasts popped out and remained exposed above the edge of her dress. As if paralyzed, the woman sat there, unable to right herself, and the rest of the guests made heroic efforts to keep their eyes fixed in the distance and to resume the conversations that had frozen in their throats. The situation was tense for a few long seconds. Suddenly, one of the many waiters serving the table, a fellow with a plate in one hand and a serving spoon in the other, stepped up and bowed.

"Will you permit me, Madame?" he asked.

The lady nodded in confusion. Suavely placing his spoon under her breast, the waiter neatly returned it to its place with a gentle flip of his wrist. A sigh of relief escaped from many at the table and everyone began to talk again with great animation. When the dinner was over, the maître d' called in the waiter in question.

"You're fired."

"But, maître, why?"

"For what you did at the table."

"I don't understand," stammered the waiter. "I have been working for you for five years and I learned my job following your instructions. Many times I have heard you sum up the waiter's job by saying that he must always endeavor to see that everything proceeds as smoothly as possible, redressing quickly and without excitement any accident that may happen. I was nearest to the lady; I had to do something, everyone else was too nervous and disturbed . . ."

GLUTTONY

"My dear friend," replied the maître d', "I am not firing you for your action, which was quite opportune, but for the way you did it. It's a matter of style, if you like, but an extremely important one."

"I don't understand."

"My good man, I refer to your spoon; you ought to have warmed it beforehand."

DRINKING TO LIVE

The tradition is ancient, and like so many French traditions, it is carefully kept up. The maxims referring to it go back for centuries and centuries.

"An ass drinks only when he is thirsty, but that's because he only drinks water." (Beroalde de Verville, 1612.)

If the seventeeth century called someone who didn't drink wine an ass, the nineteenth had a still harsher word for him.

"All the wicked drink water. This is proved by Noah's flood." (Ségur, *Chansons morales,* 1801.)

The French don't want to be either asses or wicked. On the average they drink two hundred liters of wine a year, besides seventy liters of beer and other kinds of liquor, for a total of twenty-eight liters of pure alcohol, according to the National Statistical Institute in Paris. Compared to the consumption of other countries, their twenty-eight liters lead—or follow, depending on which end of the chart you see as up—Italy's twenty liters, Germany's fourteen, and the figures for Switzerland, Belgium, England, the United States, and Denmark—all about equal—oscillating between eight and ten liters a year per capita.

Without wine no dinner is worthy of the name. Among many other unpleasant things that de Maupassant had to say about the Prussians was his comment that "they start to drink after they have eaten," which represented a total condemnation of their life style.

GLUTTONY

This difference in the consumption of alcohol shows up again when the time arrives to take the consequences. France holds the world record for cirrhosis of the liver, twelve dying of it each year for every 100,000 inhabitants, which is twice the number in Italy, three times the number in Spain, and ten times the number in England. Alcoholism is directly responsible for the deaths of 5,816 Frenchmen a year, all by itself. And this figure doesn't count its influence in arming assassins for their work: for in fact, it is estimated that half of all the violent deaths in the country can be traced to the killer's use of alcohol. These figures were published by the World Health Organization in February 1969.

All useless numbers, of course. The French continue drinking, because wine is as much a part of their lives as eating bread. And since the intelligence and work of several generations have gone into the elaboration of this vice, a great net of vested interests has been created that makes it very difficult, if not impossible, to reduce consumption by law. The most audacious leader France ever had was not de Gaulle, who gave Algeria her independence despite the objections of millions of Frenchmen; it was Mendès-France, who eulogized milk as a substitute for wine and publicly drank glasses of the bovine substance to set an example, something that in Paris seemed almost obscene. There may have been other, more political reasons, but I haven't the slightest doubt that Mendès-France's failure was seriously influenced by his defiance of the customs of his country. A good 99 per cent of all Frenchmen are linked to the alcohol industry, whether as viticulturists, waiters, bottlers, vintners, or consumers.

Drinking is living. Religion is called in to prove it.

"He who drinks good wine sees God." (*Proverbes de France*, 1556.)

"Christ didn't change wine into water, but water into wine."

There isn't an ordinary house in France in which a bottle of *rouge* or *blanc* doesn't come to the table along with the long loaf of bread. Shocked by the statistics of con-

GLUTTONY

sumption mentioned earlier, the government has taken a variety of measures, so far with but indifferent success. One regulation prohibits the sale of alcohol to minors. Another measure laid the basis for a propaganda campaign in the movie theaters. I saw one short sequence in which a few soldiers are shown on maneuvers. When they get a break, they rest in the shade of some boulders and open up bottles ... of mineral water. "Our brave soldiers," says the commentator's voice, "don't drink wine." Shouts of laughter echoed through the theater and they continue to be heard each time the film short is run.

Not long ago the National Assembly fixed the percentage of alcohol that a person may legally have in his blood; beyond that he risks going to jail. The mayor of Chateauneuf-du-Pape, cradle of the famous wine, decided that the people who turned off the highway to visit his town for the purpose of sampling the new vintage might have difficulty getting back through the police check, so he organized rest parks where the drinkers could remain under the protection and safeguard of local authorities, who would decide the appropriate moment for them safely to continue their journeys (*L'Express,* May 4, 1970).

When the French give a tip they know what it is for, or was originally. Their word for tip is *pourboire,* literally "for drinking."

A year or so ago a trial in Reims drew a lot of attention. A man was accused of having killed a girl after raping her. He was absolved of all charges, largely because a famous attorney, Isorni, a man who hadn't tried a criminal case in years, agreed to take his case after observing that the charges were based more on the enmity provoked by the personality of the accused than on solid proof. To begin with, the suspect was a Pole, with a name as harsh to French ears as Kaczmarczyk and with habits odder still. He liked solitary walks and "what was most disturbing, he drank only milk" (*France-Soir,* October 14, 1968). Capable of any crime, in short.

Wine is easily associated with love. "The wines of Burgundy are good for women, especially when they are drunk by men."

There aren't any wines on a level with the French. Once again we have the vicious circle we saw before in connection with food and fashion: the French do things well, but they promote them as if they were even better. I don't know how they have managed to convince every other country that what they make is always the very best and most elegant, but they've done it. Perhaps it's because they have applied a banker's seriousness to products that in other countries would be of relative insignificance. Put another way, the French sell their clothes and wines with the same organization and discipline that the Swedes apply to their steel.

Naturally enough, any attempt a foreigner may make to understand something about wine in France is regarded with skepticism in the best of cases, with indignation in the worst. Just as many Spaniards think that the mere fact of their nationality gives them an understanding of bullfights and flamenco, the French believe that no one on earth can dispute their right to the scepter of viticultural wisdom.

Once on an automobile trip I stopped to eat in a cold *auberge de route*. I asked for a bottle of red wine and this was produced, but it was ice cold. I complained to the *patronne* and she looked at me compassionately.

"Red wine is served at room temperature, Monsieur."

"So it is," I answered, "but the room is supposed to be warm."

It's not rare to see poetry used in praise of wine. "A day without wine is a day without sun," they say in Provence. "Les Rochers wine is velvet for the stomach," is another slogan. Other references may be made to cultural history. "Pineau," I read in a sign, "the *vin rosé* of the *déjeuner sur l'herbe.*" The advertising agency's confidence that the public would know Manet's great Impressionist painting is a good indication of the level of culture in France.

GLUTTONY

Could any definition of a perfect champagne be more lyrical than this? "The palate should first be agreeably surprised by the sparkling bubbles and a flattering, velvety taste, and then it should detect a fruity aftertaste perfuming the mouth that leaves one in a delicious meditation about the aroma of the wine for a long moment after he has put down the glass. Without this you have nothing but a wine cadaver." These emphatic words were pronounced by an emphatic lady, Clicquot's widow, "*La veuve Clicquot.*"

"Never drink water," was the caption of a French cartoon famous around the world. To demonstrate the correctness of the warning, the picture showed a boy urinating in a river.

The trouble with any success is that everyone else tries to copy it—and sometimes they succeed. Long ago French liqueurs were made in convents, where the exact proportions of the ingredients were passed from monk to monk as an important secret. Today the great wine manufacturers are open to the public and no mystery prevents anyone from making a drink very similar to the one that has achieved fame. This is now happening to champagne, which is being challenged by the production of other countries that have imitated French methods so well that every day their wine more nearly approaches their model. When they achieve their goal, the amount of champagne sent abroad by France—now an enviable 30 per cent of the total produced—will necessarily tend to fall. Some optimists point out, however, that foreign producers still work with a single vintage instead of mixing the vintages of several years to achieve a perfect result. Besides, they add, "the important thing is that the people of the world become accustomed to drinking champagne. When they have, they will wind up demanding the best, which will continue to be ours for many years. . . ."

Champagne is expensive, between $1.50 and $6 a bottle in France. Nevertheless, a popular newspaper didn't hesitate recently to give instructions about the best way to buy, keep, and drink it (*France-Soir,* December 7, 1968). Even the Frenchmen who couldn't afford such a luxury probably read the article with pleasure and emotion. The king of wines is French. What a miracle!

With what foods does champagne go best? The article could hardly have been more generous. "As an apéritif, it stimulates the appetite. But it goes well with fish, seafood, chicken, and goose. It is possibly less suitable with *pâté de foie-gras,* but all in all, it doesn't go badly with any food.

"Please don't put champagne in the freezing compartment of your refrigerator because this will 'break' the wine. Place it in the refrigerator an hour before opening it. About 45 degrees F. is cold enough. And don't freeze the glasses, either—the champagne will be extinguished." The reader might be pardoned for concluding that the subject of the article was a living being, delicate and sensitive as a fairy princess, rather than a bottle of wine.

The article continues: "Pick up the bottle carefully, and never force the cork.... When the cork is nearly out of the bottle as a result of the circular pressures applied to it, extract it little by little, so that the gas escapes slowly, with barely an audible 'pffft.'"

(The journalist didn't even mention the barbarous custom of popping the cork. What *gaucherie.*)

"The best champagne glasses are tulip-shaped with thin or hollow stems. To avoid excessive spume, tip the glass and pour the champagne in along the lower rim, righting the glass as it fills up."

The French inevitably seem to surround their merchandise with ceremonial details, and this has much to do with their success. I must repeat what I said earlier about other French exports. What gave them their triumph in the first place was the seriousness with which they themselves viewed the product, especially when other countries didn't think it important. France presents its wines, its fashions, and its cooking with the same solemnity as it does its paintings and literature. In Great Britain, no one would think to speak in the same tones about Shakespeare and

GLUTTONY

Guinness stout. But in France, Balzac and ten-year-old Burgundy receive the same emphasis, and this can sometimes produce in the customer a momentary feeling that he is out of touch. As any salesman knows, when a customer is disconcerted, his defenses are down, and all you have to do is write down his order.

Martell and Hennessy, two cognac manufacturers, are doing just that, year after year. They currently sell 90 per cent of their output abroad. England takes the most, and Germany is next.

In sum, French wines are probably the best in the world because nowhere else has anyone been able to apply so much science, work, dedication, and patience to make sure that theirs would be better. In the few instances where a French wine is not the best, France has managed to convince the world that the elegant and intelligent thing to do is to believe it anyway.

6 Envy

NATIONAL LACK OF ENVY

"In the adversities that trouble our good friends we always discover something not entirely disagreeable to ourselves."

So wrote La Rochefoucauld in 1665 and the urbanity of his phrasing removes none of the sting from his message.

Is the Frenchman envious? If envy means the desire to possess what others possess, he is. But if by envy we understand a desire to see others suffer so that we may seem by contrast to be getting along better than we are, the French aren't envious. Put another way, it seems to me that their

ENVY

egotism—a quality shared by all humans but gravely overdeveloped in the French—immunizes them, so to speak, against envy. They are so wrapped up in the pursuit of their own happiness that they don't have time to worry about or resent the happiness of anyone else.

There is, besides, another basic reason: envy arises most naturally in the dispossessed. Even though there have been cases of millionaires who wanted to snatch away the crust of bread a beggar was about to put in his mouth, it is more logical that the beggar should be the one to want what the millionaire has. A man who is poor, who suffers the discomfort of hunger and cold, may resent the existence of anyone whose stomach is full and protected against the elements by a good coat. This is the feeling of hate born of a comparison, the desire to see something bad happen to a person who seems to have all the luck. Envy, in short.

Now France, both absolutely and when compared to other European nations, is a rich country. Her fertile soil, the abundant waters that beautify and nourish her fields, and the coal mines that supply electric power to her industry have led to a collective economic well-being that is now shared by nearly everyone, thanks to the French Revolution's distribution of the property of the clergy and nobility. Generally speaking, the bourgeoisie or middle class is larger than in other countries, taking in people who would be part of the proletariat elsewhere, as well as the cream of the aristocracy, who continue to have some social prestige but no particular political or economic power.

The French bourgeoisie is very sure of itself, its work habits, its political position, and its cultural power. In the frequent marriages between nobles intent upon gilding their family shields and the daughters of well-to-do bourgeois families, the bourgeois parents are the ones who object. They don't think that a name preceded by "de" or the ruins of a castle in the Gironde are worth much, and naturally can't begin to compare with the advantages of having an honorable, hard-working son-in-law (assuming

E N V Y

that the noble, living up to his image, isn't such a man).

Considering that envy has no economic basis (since the majority of the French live comfortably) and no basis in blood (the nobility has lost its earlier prestige), it's not surprising that this sin has lost most of its effectiveness as a motive in the nation's heart. People who are well off still retain the possibility of bettering their position vis-à-vis their neighbors, by trading in their *deux chevaux* for a Simca or their Simca for a Renault, for example, but these are small steps. The French themselves regard envy as senseless, unproductive, and a waste of time. Wasting time irritates the average Frenchman more than almost anything else, since his avarice counsels him never to waste anything.

Envy may be directed at other nations and their customs, as well as at individuals. France seems free of this kind of national envy also. We have noted that the tastes of the French are nearly always satisfied by their environment. The Frenchman likes to eat well, drink well, have an apéritif with his friends, and read good books. These needs are abundantly satisfied by the society around him. Germany may have a stronger currency and produce more goods more quickly than France, but the average German can't indulge in a glass of wine with his friends before going home because the drink is too expensive, despite his high salary. Nor does he eat from such a refined menu as someone from Marseilles or Reims. Italy and Spain may have lower prices, but in some of their regions poverty is extreme. France, in contrast, has managed to keep production and consumption in nearly perfect equilibrium everywhere in the country.

The French could envy countries with higher standards of living, but they don't because such advantages seem useless to them. For example, as we mentioned earlier, official statistics show that the number of French houses that have a bathtub or even a shower is impressively small. The exact figure, 56 per cent, is surpassed by the figures for every other country in Western Europe, includ-

ENVY

ing Portugal (*L'Express,* October 12, 1970). Recently an advertising campaign was undertaken on the radio and in large-circulation magazines (I have the ads from *Jours de France* and *Paris-Match)* to convince the French just how wonderful it is to have a shower. A person who unconsciously equates being well off with being well kempt would be astonished by this advertising, which might have been concocted for the Eskimos or the inhabitants of a rain forest. "Come now, don't be stubborn, put a shower in your home. You will find that it is very pleasant, and so will your children. You say it will cost too much? Don't believe it. The state will help you foot the bill. What, you don't feel like making improvements since you don't own your apartment? [See Avarice.] This case has been taken into account also. When you put in the shower, it increases the value of the apartment, and the owner has to reimburse your expense when you leave. So don't be stubborn, friends! Put in that shower."

These startling ads expose the existence of a state of affairs that could make it easy for the French to envy the people of other countries, who may have fewer writers and artists but who live more comfortably in their homes. The fact is, however, the situation in France is not something the French couldn't help, but entirely of their own choosing. The reason France trails nearly every civilized country with respect to sanitary facilities in the home is simply that the French think that it makes no difference. Not once in discussing housing with the French has the person I was talking to ever felt the slightest twinge of embarrassment about the statistics on bathtubs. So long as a house has what they regard as the most important facility, a bidet, the rest seems superfluous.

So far we have been speaking of the average Frenchman. Exceptional intellectual refinement may open the way for new kinds of envy, along with other unhealthy passions that sometimes afflict the fellow countrymen of the author of *Les Fleurs du mal.*

The wickedest book I have ever read is not Baudelaire's

ENVY

but *Les Liaisons dangereuses* by Choderlos de Laclos, an eighteenth-century French writer. The essential evil of the work isn't rooted in the actions the characters take but in the motive that drives the two protagonists, the Marquise de Merteuil and the Viscount de Valmont. This motive is evil for the sake of evil, or better, hatred of virtue. In the letters they exchange, the protagonists lay out strategic plans and each supporting action that will produce the ruin of a maiden or the desperation of a husband. Neither is impelled along this path by love or an ambition to climb the social ladder; what they desire is to sink someone morally. (A latent sexual interest does seem to lurk in their correspondence as well. The long descriptions they give of libidinous scenes and their preparations for them excite them both. I mentioned before that the *voyeur* is a French character type now universally recognized.)

Let us look at some examples of their deviate pleasures. In the conclusion of one of her letters, the Marquise encourages the Viscount to complete his conquest of a virtuous lady. "Farewell, Viscount! Good night and good luck, but for the love of God, drive on! Think to yourself that if you fail to conquer that woman, all the others will be ashamed that they bent to your will." In the same letter she spells out the conditions under which she will again give herself to him. "As soon as you shall have had your way with that pious beauty and can give me proof of it, come and I will be yours. Arranged this way, my gift will be a reward instead of a consolation, and this idea appeals to me more. Furthermore, your triumph over that woman will be all the spicier for being an act of infidelity." As proof, she asks the Viscount for a letter from the conquered woman. "I am curious to find out what a sanctimonious prude is able to write at such a moment and to see what veil she attempts to draw over her actions after having thrown off the veils that cover her body." (Letter of August 19, 17—.)

For both lovers, the important thing is not to conquer but to destroy, especially to destroy another person's morality.

ENVY

When the Viscount is with the young woman he has seduced for purely mental pleasure, he tries to break down whatever moral principles she has left.

"The girl was happy, and to increase her happiness, in the intermissions of our lovemaking I told her all the amorous adventures I could remember; and to make them more thrilling and memorable to her, I attributed them all to her mother. My reason for this choice of a heroine was sound. It animated my timid partner and at the same time inspired her with profound disgust for her mother. Long, long ago I learned that while this stratagem is not indispensable to the successful seduction of a girl, it is an exceptionally serviceable device and sometimes the most effective of all when you are trying to lead her into depravity, because a girl who doesn't respect her mother doesn't respect herself. This moral truth seems so useful to know that I was happy to give you an example in support of the thesis." (Letter of October 11, 17—.)

For the Viscount, victory does not consist in the act of possession but in finishing off another's goodness. While planning the conquest of Madame de Tourvel, a judge's wife, he is not satisfied when, skillfully entrapped, she offers signs of submission. "My intention," he wrote his friend and confidante, "is that she feel keenly the value and extent of each sacrifice that she has to make for me. I want to see her virtue die a slow and painful death; to force her to watch this desolating spectacle without flinching; and to withhold from her the happiness of having me in her arms until I have forced her to stop dissimulating her desire. This is the least I can do to avenge myself on a woman so proud that it makes her blush to confess that she adores me." (Letter of September 11, 17—.)

The novel ends, of course, with a certain poetic justice. The conspirators quarrel and denounce each other. The Viscount dies at the hands of the young Danceny, admirer of Cécile de Volanges. The Marquise is ejected from good society, loses her money, and is made repugnant to behold by a horrible disease. Such blatant moralizing unhappily

ENVY

fails altogether to erase from the reader's imagination the incredible perversity of the protagonists, who brought to spiritual relationships the same sort of mentality that the Marquis de Sade, a contemporary of Choderlos de Laclos, applied physically to excite his libido.

ENVY IN THE PROVINCES?

Paris towers loftily over the French provinces. The Bourbon kings were determined centralists and skillfully converted the potential rivals of the throne, the principal nobles, into courtiers, taking them out of their castles and bringing them to Paris, where they were held in orbit around the king. The haughty actions of the nobles a few generations earlier, when the Guises, Montmorencys, and Montignys talked back to the king and even took up arms against him, were transformed into maneuverings in the halls of Versailles for the honor of attending the king's awakening *(le petit lever)* or having the king look upon their wives from up close. The provincial cities that might have become centers of wealth, culture, and civilization settled into a second-rate status. Paris expanded and expanded, and embellished itself with money drawn from the entire country. Today many Frenchmen boast of being Parisians even though they were born in other cities, once brilliant but today abandoned, where life comes to a halt at 9:00 P.M.

(The same pattern emerged, though to a lesser degree, in Spain, where the government's policy of centralism raised Madrid to the heights and left the word province as a synonym for smallness and boredom. The regional cities of Germany and Italy, on the other hand, are better developed: these two countries did not achieve unity until the last third of the nineteenth century, permitting music, art, and literature to flourish in every corner of the nation.

E N V Y

Today German writers, professors, and artists boast about living in Munich, Heidelberg, Cologne, and Hamburg rather than hiding the fact. Their Italian counterparts are just as proud to live in Milan, Pisa, Naples, and Palermo.)

Frenchmen in the provinces have solid grounds for feeling envy toward Paris, the capital city. Possibly as a compensation for the genuine neglect they suffer on an official level, little cities have often been selected by writers as the sites for important literary actions. Daudet *(Tartarin de Tarascon);* Flaubert *(Madame Bovary);* Stendhal *(The Red and the Black);* Balzac *(Eugénie Grandet)* and Marcel Pagnol *(Marius)* move their characters in the narrow, sad environment of the French provinces. It seems a kind of return on the glory taken away from them by Louis XIV.

"Nous avons tous la force pour supporter les maux d'autrui," said La Rochefoucauld in a famous book. But this particular strength of the French to put up with the evils of others indicates, not envy, but indifference based on the greatest sin of the French, their egotism.

The vengeance taken in other countries by someone resentful of a neighbor's happiness, occurs in France only when a person's own happiness has been disturbed. The heroine of *Bonjour, Tristesse* conspires against her father's mistress, not because she was morally offended by the relationship between the two, but because the mistress was already trying to adopt the airs of a mother and had obliged the heroine to spend her vacation studying. This is a direct and specific reaction, like that of the porcupine, who never bothers anyone so long as he is left alone, but who revenges himself with a thousand quills on anyone who bothers him. The porcupine has a better claim to being the symbol of France than the rooster.

7 Sloth

INTERMITTENT SLOTH

Tout ce qui peut être fait un autre jour ce peut être fait aujourd'hui.

                                        Montaigne, 1580.

    Deadly sins always have two aspects, one general and one particular. That is, the sin can be viewed in its essence, or it may be viewed in terms of the people who stumble into it. This second aspect is the one that changes according to the idiosyncrasies of the people.
    In the French case, it's my impression that general con-

SLOTH

cepts have value only relatively: what counts is the will of individuals to accept or reject them, as the situation demands.

Let's look at sloth. At first glance, it seems perfectly obvious that the French are not lazy. They get up early and go to bed early. Everyone in the family pitches in to help at the office, the store, or the shop. Many years before the women's liberation movement, French women were manning cannons. In Millet's famous painting which hangs over so many traditional hearths, a farm woman stands beside her husband; we know that as soon as they finish their prayer, they will both take hold of the plow or the mattock. In French gasoline stations you often see a woman hurrying out at the sound of a horn to fill a car with gasoline and oil. But there is something different about the situation from that which exists elsewhere in the world. Women who work in gas stations in other countries behave with a certain youthful lightness; there is something revolutionary and attractive about them (certainly this is so of the girls who act as gas station attendants in Madrid), and they seem to be marking out a new path. Their work seems to involve a small, lighthearted defiance of convention, as if they were saying, "You never saw a girl doing this job before, did you? But here I am, so what about it?" And they make the male jealous of his rights pardon their rebellion and pretty insolence because of their beauty, grace, and disarming smiles.

But not in France. In France the woman who comes out to fill your car with gas is a housewife, almost always fat and disheveled, who has just got up from the meal she had prepared for herself and her several children. Her apron is not meant to catch your eye but to keep her from getting covered with grease. The Frenchwoman doesn't work like a woman playing at being a man. She works like a man who has to think of the children besides.

But this total activity of all the family is drastically interrupted once a year. Restaurants and other businesses in Paris post signs during the months of August and Septem-

SLOTH

ber saying that they are closed. Many times I've noticed that no precise date is given for the reopening; the matter is left up in the air by such uncertain phrases as "at the end of the month" or "early next month." The impression one gets is that the owner may have intended this vagueness to demonstrate his complete independence. Not only does he leave when he wants to; he doesn't have to give any explanation. And as a matter of fact, the French take long vacations, longer than in other countries. The French forget about avarice and dedicate themselves to laziness.

Physical laziness, of course. The French enjoy physical laziness even in their sports, because their favorite sport is the one that causes the muscles to move least—*la pétanque,* or *bolas.* All summer long, in all the towns in France, groups of men wearing berets can be seen standing around the black metal balls on the ground, arguing. Each movement of an arm is balanced and compensated for by a thousand movements of the tongue. *Bolas* is the simplest game in the world, but to judge by the commentaries it provokes, you would think it was the most scientific. The players are also accustomed to quenching their thirst with good wine, since the game goes on in front of the café in the central plaza, usually called the Place de la République. Farmers and city dwellers play and each move is savored along with a glass of red wine or *pastis.*

Those who consider bolas too strenuous can always turn to the French relaxation *par excellence,* fishing. On the banks of the innumerable rivers in France, on her canals and dams, and on her coasts one sees everywhere the graceful image of a fisherman with his pole, smoking and looking out into space. Inevitably he has a lunch basket by his side. He seems absolutely at rest, with no connection to a wife, children, or a home. Yet the most agreeable part of the day for him comes when he opens his basket and takes out the ample, well-prepared meal packed by his wife, which he tops off with a suitable wine.

If the French are indefatigable workers they are also limitlessly able to rest. They take hold of rest as forcefully as work. But while Americans do the same thing because they don't know how to relax, and fill the free time they don't know how to use with activity—long automobile rides, eighteen holes of golf, six sets of tennis—the French just as enthusiastically throw themselves into resting. They do it better than anyone else.

Yes... the women of France work hard. So do the men. They get up early, never take a break, and go to bed exhausted. There's not a trace of laziness in them...

... while they are at work. But when the Frenchman decides the hour has come to stop, no power on earth, political, patriotic, or religious can block him from pursuing his desire for rest. When he decides to go home for lunch he slams shut the iron grating in front of his shop at the risk of pinching the hand of his best customer. Anyone who comes running up out of breath and attempts to convince him to stay open another minute is met by the bobbing head and ritornello mentioned earlier. This time the *ah, nons* are punctuated by the information that *c'est fermé*, we're closed, and sometimes the helpful clarification, *c'est comme ça*, that's the way it is. And it certainly is that way. The Frenchman finds work and rest equally sacred. No appeals to common sense or to the country's need to attract tourists will move him to stay open a few minutes longer than the time scheduled for his convenience. As I said before (in Pride), the "convenience" taken into consideration here is a purely individual or, if you prefer, family matter. In the same block one shop may open at nine and close at six, another open at eleven and close at eight. What other people think of a shop's schedule is no concern to the owner.

The large department stores are just as rigid about closing on time. A friend of mine, a Spanish lady of unmistakable distinction, was once surprised in the Galeries Lafayette by the closing hour when she had six packages in her hands and was trying to buy some merchandise to make up a seventh. Hearing the bell, a salesgirl threw a white cloth not just over the display but over my friend's

SLOTH

hand as she was feeling the quality of the goods, and disappeared. The lady announced in a clear voice that if she were to be treated thus, she was leaving everything, including what she had already charged, and a section chief came over and wrapped up her last purchase because avarice that time had more power than sloth.

This obsession of the French shows up in their love of vacations. *Les congés payés*, or vacations with pay, are relatively new in France, but nothing has been as popular since the revolution's invention of social equality. Like that achievement, the achievement of the paid vacation is vigorously defended. The average Frenchman just loves to hear someone complain that he was in a shop and nobody was there. "We also have a right to rest, don't we?" The *on a bien le droit* packs quite a moral clout.

(They are also capable of resting when something interests them more than earning money. I know this from my personal experience. My car once broke down and when I edged into a garage in the nearest town, the attendants were sitting with their ears glued to a radio and didn't even glance at me. They were listening to a rebroadcast of a section of the Tour de France and until the cyclists arrived at the finish no one paid any attention to me.)

The French nation has found room for at least one professional practitioner of sloth. He is the bum, or *clochard,* whose typical silhouette can so often be seen next to the Seine. As the French have done with so many other things, they have sold this type of vagabond to the world, just as they sell the designs and concoctions of their dressmakers, cooks, and writers. Everywhere else in the world a bum is simply a man who refuses to work and prefers to beg. But the French manage to be original even on the bottom rung of their social ladder. The *clochard,* first of all, almost never begs for money. When he is lying down or sitting, wrapped up in his rags against the chill of the air, he hardly deigns to look at the citizens who pass near him, and of course he tries to have nothing to say to them. He lives on food and clothing that have been thrown out,

SLOTH

and he sometimes passes through the markets, where he is recognized and given leftovers.

Now and then during the summer he may help harvest some crop in the country. He needs little and he has what he needs. Within the bounds of his mean existence, he is a genuine philosopher. Unable to escape the world around him by going up, the way the rich do who isolate themselves in palaces defended by guards and dogs, he has headed downward, separating himself just as completely from a society that disgusts him. His walls are his rags; his guards and dogs are the fear that people have that he harbors evil intentions toward them. Nobody bothers him and he generally doesn't bother anyone else.

Sometimes he is in jail, but only because he wants to be. When the winter promises to be too harsh, he presents himself at the police station as a vagrant and as such, an outlaw. The police, with exquisitely rigorous French logic, lock him up, knowing the motives that have brought him in. The representatives of law and order really have nothing against him, for they know that he is one more element making up the great variety of Paris, and that as many tourists come looking for him as for the nudes of the Folies Bergère or the terraces of the Champs-Élysées.

But the *clochard* manages something very difficult to achieve in hard-working France: he is the champion of sloth. Long may he prosper, and may poets and writers sing his praises.